America is Now a Socialistic Country

John D. Rigazio

authorHOUSE®

AuthorHouse™
1663 Liberty Drive
Bloomington, IN 47403
www.authorhouse.com
Phone: 1-800-839-8640

First published by AuthorHouse 8/24/2010

ISBN: 978-1-4520-6587-8 (sc)
ISBN: 978-1-4520-6591-5 (hc)
ISBN: 978-1-4520-6586-1 (e)

Library of Congress Control Number: 2010911935

Printed in the United States of America

This book is printed on acid-free paper.

Contents

DEDICATION

This book is dedicated to Kelly McKenna, without whom I couldn't have put my memoirs into book form; the good Lord, who kept me alive while dealing with my diabetes and depression; all of the local readers of my political column, **National Politics is Everybody's Business**; and to my father and mother, who were both born in Italy but were the greatest Americans I ever knew. I have devoted two chapters of my new book to my parents.

Thank you,

John Donald Rigazio

PREFACE

I, John Donald Rigazio, ran for President of the United States in the 2004 NH primaries against President Bush and 13 others.

I never had any political aspirations; however, I wanted to stop the growth of socialism in America.

I have listed my interviews, ads, and political positions on the war in Iraq and the false economy. You will see the foresight I had in 2004, and that many of the same problems are still with us.

I am sorry the book has little order and some chapters should be rewritten. However, that being said, please read this book. I have been writing a column (*National Politics is Everybody's Business*) for over seven years now and have a large following in the local newspapers.

One thing is for sure, the Republicans, Democrats, so called Liberals, and so called Conservatives will all have to become Nationalists if we want to go back to the America we once knew.

It's apparent that the extreme left is trying to take over the Democratic Party and the extreme right is trying to take over the Republican Party. The two-party system in America is being controlled by the large American (in name only) world-wide corporations who want to continue making goods as cheap as possible world-wide, selling as high as possible in America and paying as little taxes as possible.

If we Americans are Independents and/or Undeclared we must vote for the person, not the party, who represents the best interests of America and the American people.

Getting involved in the primary elections is very important because with all its faults, the two-party system is the only game in town.

INTRODUCTION

If America is going to maintain our national sovereignty and control our own economic destiny, we must recognize the path which globalization is leading us on. If allowed to continue, *unfair* world trade will lower the standard of living for the majority of us Americans.

As more and more Americans cannot provide for themselves, other hard-working taxpayers will be forced to pay much higher taxes at the city, state and federal level, thus changing our democracy to a socialistic government. While we didn't vote for socialism at the ballot box, that's what we are going to get because of our fiscal irresponsibility.

If we go one step further, socialism enforced by state and federal government troops is communism, isn't it?

When Obama was sworn in in January 2009, America was in a full blown recession/depression. Why I state recession and depression is that many Americans will be in this recession period; however, more and more Americans who cannot put food on the table, pay their rent or mortgage, put gas in their gas tank, pay their oil heating bills, and pay their ever increasing city, state and federal taxes will be in a depression.

The old saying is it's a recession when your *neighbor* is out of work, but it's a depression when *you* are out of work. As the recession pushes more and more of us Americans into a depression, the recession will last years and the violence in America's cities will escalate.

There are many things America must do as soon as possible. The first is to look out for our best interests first, and the world's second. Then we must bring the trade deficit down to zero or as near zero as possible. The American economy cannot continue providing the world economy with good paying jobs at our expense.

Let me see now; they tell us a weak dollar made our exports cheaper all over the world market and world products higher on the American market. I see a weak dollar for years to come, so why can't we get a zero balance on trade? We in America must stop our deficit spending, balance our federal budget, and start paying down our national debt; we must push for a zero trade deficit. Our present American economy is unsustainable.

The American people will soon realize that George W. Bush not only handled the Iraq War wrong from beginning to end but his policy of "deficits don't matter" has bankrupted the country.

Nothing much has changed since my first book was published in July of 2008. Our country has let large (American in name only) corporations buy and manufacture goods as cheap as possible worldwide and sell for as high as possible in America, while paying as little taxes as possible.

The French have a saying, "The more things change, the more they remain the same."

Until America can put the American economy first and the world economy second, we will experience more and more socialism in our American political system. It is the cancerous growth of socialism which is destroying what made us the greatest country in the world.

1

BY THE END OF 2010, OUR FEDERAL DEBT PROBLEM WILL BECOME A CRISIS

Published 2/27/10

We have this year, 2010, to restore confidence to the foreign countries, worldwide investors and our fellow Americans who are holding our federal bonds and treasury notes. The way things look now, the question about America's soon-to-be $14.3 trillion debt is that it doesn't look good for investors. In fact, most think it isn't *if* America's financial debt problem will reach a crisis stage it is *when*.

I predict that unless America can show the world we are taking corrective steps to balance our budget and start paying down our debt, all our lenders will sell our treasury bonds and notes and not hold the American dollar. If we have nothing to back up our dollar and we keep printing more, we will see runaway inflation in America.

This lengthy article is going to offer some suggestions which will help us curb spending, and most importantly, grow revenues.

Cutting spending when the need for social spending is growing rapidly and indiscriminately raising taxes on America's lower and middle income Americans is counter-productive. As we all realize, putting Americans back to work is the way to grow revenues (this is not going to happen in 2010 unless we get *fair world trade* agreements that are *enforced*.)

Also, we must provide poor and lower income Americans with the incentive to join the workforce. To do this, we must increase the minimum wage by $3 an hour. There has to be a greater difference between what a person gets for working and what they receive for *not* working.

We must stop the Senate and House health care reform bills. While we provide health care for 45 to 50 million non-insured citizens and illegal immigrants, we are mandating *all health care costs* be paid for by big and small business. This is going to *add to unemployment* in 2010, 2011, 2012 and 2013. When we are trying to create jobs in America, this is highly counter-productive to *job growth*.

I don't think the politicians in Washington (Republicans *and* Democrats) have the intestinal fortitude (guts) to initiate the tax increases which will be needed to balance our budget and allow us to start paying down our debt.

As the Republicans have done since 1980, we have not advocated a large federal tax hike since Bush Senior said "Read my lips" (no tax increases). He did increase taxes and, of course, became a one-term president. So to get elected to Washington, you must listen to the public, tell them what they want to hear, and in the next sentence tell them you are not going to raise taxes.

This is what Karl Rove told two-term President George W.: "Don't raise taxes … deficits *don't matter.*"

To the American people (this includes disgruntled conservative Republicans who are trying to make a political statement with their "Tea Party" tax revolts) I say: Where were you when George W. put America in debt to the tune of $6 trillion? Yes, Tea Party people, deficits *do* matter and we have to pay that debt *plus* interest. There is no free lunch and there is no free money.

The old Republican war cry of "Cut spending and cut taxes" is not the answer. However, will Americans vote for someone who says "We are going to raise your taxes"? I don't think so. (Remember Presidential candidate George McGovern, who honestly said he would have to raise taxes? He didn't win one state.)

To balance our federal budget we will need tax increases; however, these tax increases will hurt the economy if they increase the need for social spending.

The globalization of the American economy and the American financial system itself is in the best interests of the world economy first and the American economy second. The legislation needed in 2010 to restore confidence to our lenders that we will balance our budget and start paying down our debt will require us to put America first and the world economy second.

Have we got enough of our national sovereignty left to control our own economic destiny? Briefly, here is what needs to be done.

JOB GROWTH

We all know we need to put Americans back to work if we are going to balance our federal budget. Until we get out of the World Trade Organization (WTO) and insist on fair trade agreements we will not get job growth in our economy.

INCREASE THE MINIMUM WAGE BY $3 PER HOUR

This would increase the taxes paid to state and federal government. It would help the growth of the economy because 100 percent of the $3 per hour increase will go straight into consumer spending, which is two-thirds of our economy. It will save the states hundreds of thousands of dollars that is now needed to *subsidize* American workers who are not being paid a living wage.

This $3 per hour increase in the minimum wage would provide an *incentive* for Americans on welfare to join the workforce.

We cannot let the National Chamber of Commerce fight every proposed hike in the minimum wage as if it were going to cause runaway inflation or ignite labor unions to demand higher wages and benefits. Believe me, union workers are more worried about job security than wage and benefit increases. Although along with the $3 per hour increase in the minimum wage we can institute a federal wage freeze on all union workers' pay. It is way past time we let non-union workers' pay increase to a living wage.

In my opinion, the National Chamber of Commerce is a tool of big business to get cheap labor which needs to be subsidized by the taxpayers.

A $3 per hour increase in the minimum wage would increase tax revenues, decrease safety net spending, and spur consumer spending. It is a win, win, win situation.

HEALTH CARE REFORM

The current health care bill in the Senate and House will be a job killer. Let's face facts – 45 to 50 million Americans do not have health care insurance, but they do have health care. For our federal government to mandate big and small businesses to provide health insurance not only for their employees, but for the other 45 to 50 million Americans who are receiving health care but not paying for it, is ridiculous.

Both health care reform bills are socialistic boondoggles incognito. They put the cost of health care on the backs of businesses who are the very ones we look to to create job growth.

Health care, like Social Security, must be paid for directly out of *all* citizens' paychecks. We must adopt the Canadian health care system and adopt a single payer provider.

THE IRS MUST BE REPLACED

The IRS is not producing the revenues needed to grow our economy. The fact that more poor and lower income Americans pay little or no taxes and the rich and big business have tax loopholes, plus the growing number of Americans who don't even file any income taxes, compiled with many tax cheaters – it's little wonder why federal revenues are declining when they should be increasing.

We also have a growing underground economy in America as more and more Americans and illegals are dealing with cash only and not paying any income taxes. This underground economy is at least $500 billion a year.

We must have a national consumption tax (aka national volume added or national sales tax) as of Jan. 1, 2011. We can make it 10 percent on everything. Five percent of this national consumption tax goes to the federal government and five percent goes to the states to pay for the *unfunded* mandates the federal government passes.

Also, as of 2011 the IRS should cut their taxes in half and make them much more simple.

In a year or two, if the national consumer tax increases federal and state revenues, we can double it to 20 percent and nearly eliminate the IRS.

A national value added sales tax will let America receive revenues from goods sold in America by slave labor countries and eliminate the cash-only underground economy.

AMERICA NEEDS A JOB GROWTH COMMISSION

America needs a "Job Growth Commission" to ensure American workers a fair share in an unfair global marketplace, where only America practices free world trade.

2

MY FATHER, JBR: A GREAT AMERICAN

Published 1/3/08

I never went to college and I am computer illiterate. So what is it in my education that gives me the right to offer constructive criticism to our federal government on the many grave problems facing our country?

Over and above my constitutional right of freedom of speech, I hereby give you my educational background.

The first part of my education was strong parental guidance; secondly, I was drafted and spent two years (November 1952 to November 1954) in the U.S. Army Infantry, which was an education in itself. I was a businessman for 50 years in the wholesale/retail food business, dealing with the biggest business in the U.S. I watch all the TV news and financial channels, and I read one or more newspapers every day.

Perhaps my greatest education on what it means to be an American came from a great American (my father), John Batista Rigazio, who passed away in 1949. I was 17 and had just graduated from Spaulding High.

My father was the only person in his family who came over from Italy as a teenager. He was 58 when he died. He worked in the brickyards and later opened three retail fruit and produce businesses, plus one wholesale produce route. He himself spoke three languages fluently; however, he would not allow my mother to teach us Italian.

In his mind, we were Americans of Italian descent, not Italians living in America. He ingrained many American values in me which are too many to list. However, the one I could never forget was America was the land of opportunity, not the land of guarantee.

So in 1964, I was a 33-year-old businessman and family man and never wrote a letter to the editor; never questioned my federal government's decisions. However, that all changed when Lyndon Baines Johnson (LBJ) gave his inaugural speech. He said, in essence, America was a nation of unprecedented wealth. He listed many of our great assets.

He then said amongst all this wealth we in America still had citizens living in poverty, citizens not being able to afford a college education, some not having adequate health care, and last but not least, our older citizens were in need of federal programs to take care of them.

What LBJ said in his 1964 inaugural speech was he was *guaranteeing* all Americans everything because they were Americans.

My father, John Batista Rigazio (JBR), told me America was the land of *opportunity,* not the land of guarantee.

From 1964 (the year I lost my marbles) I have been following our country's building on the 1964/68 socialistic foundation laid out by LBJ and his Great Society programs.

There is no way in a letter to the editor I could give readers my views of America's 1964 march to socialism. I will say, however, that we have more people dependent upon government to maintain their living standards. This is a direct result of trying to change America from the land of opportunity to the land of guarantee.

I suppose in retrospect if America could socialize on a balanced budget it would be OK. However, as President Reagan said, "A government big enough to give you everything you want is big enough to take everything you've got."

Note: LBJ, from 1964-68, passed 450 socialistic bills, laying down the foundation for socialistic growth in America. I feel about 150 bills were probably needed and many existing laws needed to be enforced.

He meant well; however, my father (JBR) knew you cannot change America from the land of opportunity to the land of guarantee.

3

I WAS BLESSED TO HAVE SUCH PARENTAL GUIDANCE

*Published in **The Rochester Courier, 1950***

When the Golden Rule Foundation was casting about for candidates for "The Mother of the Year," they overlooked one very imminent possibility in the person of Lena Rigazio, mother of three and a woman to whom the American ideal of democracy is a never-ending source of wonder and delight.

BORN IN ITALY

Born in the lovely old medieval town of Cigliano in Northern Italy, Mrs. Rigazio came to the United States as a girl of six years and settled with her family in Haverhill, Mass. She attended the Haverhill schools, and when she had completed her formal education was employed as a sample stitcher in one of the great shoe manufacturing plants there.

During her years in Haverhill she met John Rigazio, who was just starting a fruit business in Rochester, and they were married on Sept. 18, 1926. They took an apartment owned by the late Lena Morrison on Summer Street and Mrs. Rigazio remembers that Mrs. Morrison gave her an acquaintance party in which all the neighbors took part. Among the guests were Mrs. Dorothy Lyons, wife of the present Mayor C. Wesley Lyons, and her sister, Mrs. Marion Ross, and she has always been grateful for their friendliness and aid in making acquaintances.

BUILT LARGE BUSINESS

Both Mr. and Mrs. Rigazio became naturalized American citizens as soon as possible after settling in Rochester and together they built a wholesale and retail fruit business that today covers a wide area in southeastern New Hampshire. John, a cheerful, honest man, made friends readily and held them. Mrs. Rigazio did the bookkeeping for the business and between times raised three fine children. The two sons, Raymond and John, both graduated from Spaulding High School and the daughter, June, is a junior at Holy Rosary High.

Raymond, or "Butch" as he is known, was a football ace at Spaulding and on the death of his father last year took over the management of the business with the assistance of his mother. John is associated with them in the enterprise.

The thing that most of Mrs. Rigazio's friends will remember about her probably will be her eyes and her smile. Her lovely brown eyes reflect the kindliness of a great soul and her smile has made her the friend of hundreds of people. A deeply religious woman, she has always found comfort in her church, and the peace she has found there has been reflected so many times in the cheerfulness with which she greets everyone.

LOVES AMERICA

Mrs. Rigazio has known many sorrows, but the deep goodness that is inherent in her disposition has made her known and loved by all with whom she has made friends. And through all the years since she first came to these shores, she has never ceased to wonder at the opportunities which are available to any person who is willing to work hard, honor their God and their fellow men.

4

EXPLAINING SOCIALISM

Published 5/12/10

My friend and classmate wrote a May 10th Community Commentary in *Foster's* telling us how he feared socialism.

Yes, Mr. Lovejoy, we (you and I) have much to fear from the socialistic government that we now have. While we Americans didn't vote for socialism, that is what's being forced upon us because of our federal government's fiscal irresponsibility.

Socialism is the cancer which has America's free enterprise system in intensive care. Will the system which made America the land of opportunity survive?

You see, George, we didn't get socialized overnight and we will not get de-socialized overnight. I have been watching the growth of socialism in America for 50 years now. I won't go back any further than that. I will let that nut (or should I call him a fruitcake?) Glenn Beck call the growth of socialism a designed progressive conspiracy.

Here is how socialism grew in America. Since 1960, more and more Americans needed more and more taxpayers' money to make their living. Today, the growing number of poor and lower income (working poor) need other taxpayers' money to supply them with the very basic necessities of life.

So by taxing the middle income and higher income Americans more, many middle income Americans go into the working poor group and many higher income Americans drop down into the middle income group.

Excessive taxation is adding to socialism as our federal government has made welfare a standard of living, and the growing number of illegals who have to be subsidized by the taxpayers also pours oil on the burning fires of socialism in America.

Plus the two growth industries in America – health care and education – are in themselves socialistic, as more and more Americans cannot afford either.

I suppose if all the socialistic programs in America were financed on a balanced budget we would not have a $14 trillion deficit today. However, if we had taxed the people for the growth of socialism in America we would have elected truly conservative politicians who would have balanced the budget (like Clinton did).

Even though most Americans don't understand and don't want a socialistic system in America, we are going to have to live with it.

The greatest problem we will have is the crisis the federal deficit is going to present us in November and December of this year. On Sept. 30, our 2010 budget will end, carrying with it not a $1.6 trillion federal deficit but a $2 trillion budget deficit. The deficit stimulus spending to bring unemployment down will actually add to the unemployment rate to bring it between 11 and 12 percent.

If America does not balance its budget and present our lenders with a realistic austerity budget that instills confidence, we will have to print more money with nothing behind it. In a few years, this will cause runaway inflation and more and more socialistic growth in America.

5

AFGHANISTAN?

Published January 2010

(This article by Fred Hall Jr., an 89-year-old Rotary Club member, has changed my thinking on Afghanistan. I concur with his article 100 percent and with his permission I have included it in my book.)

To the Editor:

What happens in Iraq happens. We still have about 120,000 troops cooped up there.

What happens in Afghanistan?

The country is a third larger than Iraq, about the size of Texas; population 28 million. Tribal, primitive and mostly illiterate. The north is difficult mountain terrain. The south is an arid plain.

In 2001 we invaded under a UN coalition to oust the Taliban rulers, destroy al Qaeda and get Bin Laden. It has been a U.S. war from the beginning. We installed a puppet government under Karzai which is corrupt. The Taliban mounted an insurgency to recapture the country and we have been fighting them in piecemeal fashion ever since. Bin Laden and al Qaeda have been long gone. Al Qaeda is hydra headed – it disappears in one place and pops up in another. Afghanistan is a black hole. The more we commit to it the more difficult it will be to leave.

We already have 68,000 there with 30,000 more on the way (that's the population of Rochester). A city is being built to house the new troops. The country is landlocked. Supplies have to come through other countries, subject to pilferage and destruction – a logistical nightmare. The Taliban controls most of the countryside. The counter insurgency is to gain control of more of the countryside, and defeat the Taliban, giving the Karzai government time to build a security force capable of protecting the country.

Wishful thinking.

Karzai is corrupt. He only exists because of the dollars we give him. Take away the dollars and he disappears. The President calls him to clean up the corruption. (America would be better off if the President turned his attention to cleaning up the corruption in and out of Washington.)

We have another 70,000 people in Afghanistan. There is a UN delegation, a NATO force which with some exceptions provides lukewarm support, contractors, administrators, advisers and others.

What happens to them?

Is this really a war of necessity or just a war?

Forgotten in all of this are the volunteer Army and Marine Corps and their civilian soldier counterparts. These forces were never intended or prepared for a protracted war. The repeated deployments have created severe strains. There are serious morale and staffing problems. The family and economic disruptions have created many problems for the military and civilian families. Is our national security really at stake in Afghanistan as we look at the world around us?

Fred W. Hall Jr., Rochester

More about Fred Hall Jr.

World War II campaigner

To the Editor:

Fred Hall Jr., 89, is a highly civilized, modest, self-effacing man. He's the antithesis of a self-promoter, so many people may not be aware of his unusually extensive and valuable contributions to his community, state and nation.

A Rochester attorney for over 60 years, Fred is a former president of the NH Bar Association, has served as a member and chairman of the UNH board of trustees, as chairman of the directors of a large area bank, and as a civilian aide to the Secretary of the Army, as well as being an indefatigable advocate for countless other causes that benefit others.

In World War II, Fred served for over five years as an officer in the 1st Infantry Division, the fabled unit so hated and feared by the Germans. Fred participated in eight campaigns in Africa, Sicily, Normandy and Western Europe. His separation papers document three years, two months, and fifteen days of hazardous exposure, in addition to intensive and dangerous training time.

In 1988, the eminent military historian, Steven V. Ambrose, asked Fred to submit an oral account of his experiences on D-Day. In his books, Ambrose mentioned Fred frequently, and urged him to prepare a wide-ranging account. Fred responded with his marvelous *A Memoir of World War II,* an enthralling 50-page unvarnished record enriched by numerous cogent personal insights and observations. Copies may be found in the Rochester Library and the Rochester Historical Society building. Additional interesting material was featured in the AP news reports by war correspondent Don Whitehead. By reading the papers, Fred's mother was able to confirm he was still alive, since Fred was rather too busy to write.

Recently, Fred wrote a graphic and extremely moving five page recollection of June 6, 1944. A captain at the time, Fred was the Operations Officer of the 2nd Battalion 16th Infantry Regiment of the 1st Division, the unit selected to lead the assault on Omaha Beach.

Fred prepared the battle plan for his battalion and his *A Tale of Adversity and Audacity* is his unique perspective of that fateful day. My next letter will contain excerpts.

Jake M. Collins, Rochester

6

FIVE INCOME GROUPS

Published 7/26/07

For years now the media has been telling us Americans we are either poor, middle class or rich. First of all, there is no class system in America. Any American citizen can be born poor and still become rich. Second, if the media insists on segregating us Americans according to our incomes, let's do it right.

Yes, the poor can be put into one group and the rich can be put into another group. But the rest of us Americans *cannot* be put into one group called the middle class. Under this false terminology, a family making $50,000 a year and a family making $500,000 a year could fall under America's middle class. Get the picture? This is too much of a discrepancy in incomes to call all of us *middle class.* So, if the media wants to separate us Americans according to our incomes, let's do it right.

First of all, we have the *poor* families who make $10,000 to $20,000 a year; then we have the *lower income* families who make $20,000 to $40,000 a year; then we have the *middle income* families making $40,000 to $100,000 a year; then we have the *higher income* families making $100,000 to $500,000 a year; and then there are the *rich families* who can live on their interest for the rest of their lives, and their children and grandchildren will be born wealthy.

One of the things that always bothered me about classifying all of us Americans as middle class was that the media called some of us *higher middle class,* so some of us have to be called *lower middle class.*

Take it from me, I have seen many so-called *upper* middle class who have *no class* at all, and I have seen so-called *lower* middle class work two jobs, accept no government programs and bring up their families to obey the laws of the land. *These lower class families have class.*

So what we have to do in America is provide the *poor* with the opportunity to provide for themselves and their family, and for the *lower income* families to remain self-sufficient and try to climb the ladder to middle income status, and for the *middle income* families to maintain their status and strive to become *higher income* families, and for the higher income to maintain their higher living standards, which pay the most taxes and purchase the most goods and services. For the rich, I say take that tax cut and invest in America to create jobs. Investing in foreign countries may increase your bottom line, but you will be like the winners of a poker game on the Titanic.

By the way, the Titanic is America and the iceberg is right on course with our economy.

No, the rich are not getting any richer and the poor are not getting any poorer; however, the *lower income, middle income* and *higher income* American families are working two and three jobs just to maintain their standard of living. By the way, they are fighting a losing battle as more and more Americans are going down the economic ladder instead of going up the economic ladder. We must *reverse* this trend.

In this commentary I use the term "family incomes" as we all know it takes two paychecks for the majority of Americans to maintain our standard of living. Also, the suggested incomes in the columns are gross amounts, not take-home pay. So there are no middle class; however, we still can call our paycheck *take home pay* for after Uncle Sam takes out the taxes the only place you can go with your pay is home.

7

SIR JAMES GOLDSMITH WAS AHEAD OF HIS TIME

Published October 2003

In 1993, Sir James Goldsmith wrote a book entitled *The Trap.* This book was a #1 BEST SELLER IN FRANCE IN 1993. The book tells in DETAIL how the large multinational corporations were going to GLOBALIZE WORLD TRADE.

It's 10 years since *The Trap* was written and everything written in *The Trap* is forecasted 100 percent correctly. I call my copy of *The Trap,* which I have had for 10 years, MY BIBLE ON GLOBALIZATION and the CONSEQUENCES we the American people will have to pay when they bang the FINAL NAIL IN THE COFFIN CALLED GLOBALIZATION.

Last week, when President Bush visited France, there was an ANTI-GLOBALIZATION DEMONSTRATION in France which drew 20,000 people. We saw it for about FIVE SECONDS on national TV.

Make no mistake about it, when the WTO (World Trade Organization) sanctions the closing of a French manufacturing plant to BE RELOCATED in China or Vietnam, the French will take to the streets and totally paralyze the whole French economy.

What are we doing in America while the multinational corporations are taking away our manufacturing and high tech jobs? We are just sitting back and watching until we become a 100 percent service industry economy. Well, I for one AM MAD AS HELL AND I AM NOT GOING TO TAKE IT ANYMORE. That's why I am RUNNING FOR PRESIDENT OF THE UNITED STATES.

I AM REPRINTING TWO QUESTIONS ASKED TO GOLDSMITH IN 1993.

Who will be the losers and who will be the winners under a system of global free trade?

The losers will, of course, be those people who become unemployed as a result of production being moved to low-cost areas. There will also be those who lose their jobs because their employers do not move offshore and are not able to compete with cheap imported products. Finally, there will be those whose earning capacity is reduced following the shift in the sharing of value-added away from labor.

The winners will be those who can benefit from an almost inexhaustible supply of very cheap labor. They will be the companies who move their production off-shore to low-cost areas; the companies who can pay lower salaries at home; and those who have capital to invest where labor is cheapest, and who as a result will receive larger dividends. But they will be like the winners of a poker game on the *Titanic.* The wounds inflicted on their societies will be too deep, and brutal consequences could follow.

The new phenomenon of our age is the emergence of transnational corporations, with the ability to move production at will anywhere in the world, in order to systematically benefit from lower wages wherever they are to be found. Transnational corporations now account for one-third of global output; their global annual sales have reached $4.8 trillion, which is greater than total international trade. The largest 100 multinational corporations control about one-third of all foreign direct investment. The globalization of the market is vital to them, both to produce cheaply and to sell universally. Because they do not necessarily owe allegiance to the countries where they operate, there is a divorce between the interests of the transnational corporations and those of society.

You must remember that one of the characteristics of developing countries is that a small handful of people control the overwhelming majority of the nation's resources. It is these people who own most of their nation's industrial, commercial and financial enterprises and who assemble the cheap labor which is used to manufacture products for the developed world. Thus, it is the poor in the rich countries who will subsidize the rich in the poor countries. This will have a serious impact on the social cohesion of nations.

What are your thoughts about the World Trade Organization?

That is the organization which is supposed to replace GATT, regulate international trade, and lead us to global economic integration. It is yet another international bureaucracy whose functionaries will be largely autonomous. They report to over 120 nations and therefore, in practice, to nobody. Each nation will have one vote out of 120. Thus, America and every European nation will be handing over ultimate control of its economic destiny to an unelected, uncontrolled group of international bureaucrats.

WAKE UP, AMERICANS, LET'S NOT LET THE LARGE MULTINATIONAL CORPORATIONS CONTROL OUR OWN ECONOMIC DESTINY.

I will be putting my message on the Internet and I will SPEAK at any Democratic Party convention and I am also available to speak at ANY civic organization. PLEASE HELP ME in sending my message: "STOP GLOBALIZATION before we Americans have a much LOWER standard of living, increased taxation, less and less freedoms, and internal revolutions in many American cities."

8

CHINA DOESN'T DESERVE MOST FAVORED NATION STATUS

Published 4/22/08

Most-favored-nation (MFN) status offers low tariffs and treats countries as normal trading partners.

Termination of China's MFN status would result in duty increases on about 95 percent of U.S. imports from China. The cost effect of the increases would vary among the various product groups, but would on the whole be substantial.

In view of the overall substantial differences between the concessional (MFN) and full rates of duty, it is clear that the termination of China's MFN status would result in substantial increases in the cost of imports from China. Based on our survey of the 87 individual items whose imports in 1995 exceeded $100 million each and whose total accounted for $23.2 million (51 percent) of all U.S. imports from China in that year, the termination of China's MFN status would increase the average importers' cost of Chinese products by some 35 percent, in most individual instances between 25 and 65 percent.

Despite a strained relationship after China's 1989 crackdown of protestors in Tiananmen Square, China has been granted a MFN waiver every year since 1980.

THE MAIN REASON WHY THE U.S. MUST WITHDRAW CHINA'S MOST FAVORED NATION STATUS

No, it is not their human rights records, or their unfair trade practices, or unfair manipulation of their currency to increase their exports to America while extracting cash from our economy.

China must go because they sold Pakistan the nuclear supplies it needed to have atomic weapons.

We pay Pakistan $12 billion a year to fight off the terrorists in Southern Pakistan; however, the $12 billion is not being used for that.

Osama Bin Laden and Al Qaeda have a sanctuary in Southern Pakistan where they terrorize Afghanistan and America cannot go into Pakistan to bomb them or disrupt their training.

Why is this? The Pakistani government will not let America go after the terrorists in Southern Pakistan because Pakistan has nuclear weapons supplied to them by China.

This is the main reason the U.S. must not resume its MFN status with China next year.

Will this action bring on a trade war with China? Probably yes; however, better sooner than later – they need us as much as we need them. It's the price we have to pay to maintain our national sovereignty and to control our own economic destiny.

9

CHINA'S MOST FAVORED NATION STATUS MUST END NOW

Published 9/3/09

It's not Thanksgiving yet; however, it is way past time when we Americans start to talk "turkey" with the Chinese.

Termination of China's MFN status would result in duty increases on about 95 percent of U.S. imports from China. The cost effect of the increases would vary among the various product groups, but would on the whole be substantial.

In view of the overall substantial differences between the concessional (MFN) and full rates of duty, it is clear that the termination of China's MFN status would result in substantial increases in the cost of imports from China. Based on a survey of the 87 individual items whose imports in 1995 exceeded $100 million each and whose total accounted for $23.2 million (51 percent) of all U.S. imports from China in that year, the termination of China's MFN status would increase the average importer's cost of Chinese products by some 35 percent, in most individual instances between 25 and 65 percent.

Despite a strained relationship after China's 1989 crackdown of protestors in Tiananmen Square, China has been granted a MFN waiver every year since 1980.

1989 TO 2009 = 20 YEARS

Our U.S. Congress is so DUMB they don't even know what the Most Favored Nation (MFN) law gives China – a huge trade advantage over America.

China, with their slave labor workforce, DOES NOT NEED Most Favored Nation status to have a very favorable trade advantage over America.

So instead of the U.S. receiving a 25 to 65 percent tariff, China has been devaluing their currency by 40 percent for years. (Just recently, China lowered the devaluation of their currency to 21 percent.) This move was to meet competition for America's market from the Vietnamese. (World-wide corporations have built new, modern factories in Vietnam, where they work for less than $1.00 per hour.)

Anyway, to get back to the Chinese, they don't need MFN status to sell in America. So they ship us $200 billion plus each year, which helps their economy, and they devalue their currency so they get the money which the U.S. should get.

It amounts to about $80 billion a year the Chinese extract from America because they DEVALUE THEIR CURRENCY. So they take our jobs with lower prices and lower quality exports to America but they also take our tariff money because of their MFN status. Now to add insult to injury, they lend us back our own $80 billion a year and collect interest on it.

I WILL TALK TURKEY TO CHINA SO OUR (RIP VAN WINKLE) CONGRESS CAN CONTINUE SLEEPING

So I say to China: YOUR MOST FAVORED NATION STATUS IS STOPPED IMMEDIATELY.

Also, if China wants to continue exporting $200 billion worth of goods to America year after year they must import $200 billion from America each year.

China must be made to realize trade is a two-way street and that you get out of a garden what you put into it. If China continues to harvest our garden without putting back into it, there will be less and less to harvest.

I HAVE A QUESTION FOR CHINA

Just who will let China export billions of dollars worth of goods each year like America receives from China? Is it going to be Japan, South Korea, Europe, Russia? The answer is no country except the United States of America is going to take the quantity of Chinese exports that China needs to grow.

So, China – no more MFN, no more devaluation of your currency, and you must make America a Most Favored Nation and start bringing in our American-made cars, technology, etc.

So, China – you play ball with us or we'll have to play hardball with you. THE SOFTBALL GAME IS OVER!

10

WE MUST BARGAIN FOR FAIR TRADE WITH CHINA FROM A POSITION OF STRENGTH

Previously Published

We must bargain for FAIR TRADE with China from a POSITION OF STRENGTH. OUR STRENGTH IS OUR $14 TRILLION ECONOMY.

China and every other country in the world wants a piece of our ECONOMY. This FACT is one of the main reasons that CANCELING CHINA'S MOST FAVORED NATION STATUS will NOT cause inflation in America. They (China) will sharpen their pencil to keep their prices down to compete with every other country in the world who wants a favorable trade advantage with America.

With the rise of Vietnam as a slave labor supplier to America, we have other third world countries who will compete with China for our business. We also have Japan, South Korea, India and the emerging European nations, and the whole European community, who will compete in price for America's business.

Will taking China's MFN status away from them bring on inflation in America? The answer is NO WAY.

The book definition of inflation is TOO MUCH money chasing TOO FEW goods and services. Well, we all know the American consumer does NOT have too much money.

So for the politicians in Washington and the college professors (who never had any business experience) to tell us that taking away China's Most Favored Nation status will push prices much higher and cause inflation is TOTALLY FALSE.

These politicians and professors are the same NUMB-NUTS who tell us Americans we are engaging in "FREE WORLD TRADE."

Anyone, like me, who wants world trade but wants FAIR world trade is called a PROTECTIONIST.

In 2003, on the front page of *USA Today* newspaper, then millionaire (now billionaire) Wilbur E. Ross said, "The World Trade Organization (WTO) is a WEALTH TRANSFER ORGANIZATION not in the BEST INTEREST of America, and the flaw in free world trade is THAT ONLY AMERICA PRACTICES IT."

Anyone who has ever put together a puzzle knows you put the big parts down first and the smaller parts fit in later. China is the BIG PART of America's economic CRISIS.

When we stop their MFN status, stop them from DEVALUING their currency and make them IMPORT from America the same amount they export to America, we will have laid down the big parts of America's economic puzzle and the rest of the parts of the world economic puzzle will be SOLVABLE.

THE WEALTH OF A COUNTRY IS THEIR BALANCE SHEET AND THE NUMBER OF GOOD JOBS THEY CAN PROVIDE FOR THEIR CITIZENS.

A person with a good job is WEALTH to the country in which they live. They pay the most taxes, they purchase the most goods and services, and they don't need government welfare or safety net programs. Because of unfair trade policies, America is losing its wealth.

11

HEALTH CARE BILL IS NOT FUNDED

Published 1/7/10

President Obama said, "This health care legislation will be the greatest legislation since Roosevelt passed the Social Security Act."

However, *unlike* Social Security, it is an unfunded mandate which exceeds the ability of big and small businesses to pay for.

It is a socialistic boondoggle incognito.

It is my opinion that big business and small business cannot afford to pay for health insurance for the many Americans whom they employ. The health care bill will cause more unemployment in America.

12

AMERICA'S SEMI-SOCIALISTIC HEALTH CARE SYSTEM IS THE BEST IN THE WORLD... HOWEVER, WE CAN'T AFFORD IT.

Published 1/14/10

In the decade of the 1970s, we had 10 straight years of inflation. This prompted some columnists to write: "Saying we have a little bit of inflation is like a woman saying she is a little bit pregnant."

Saying that the current semi-socialistic health care system is not socialized medicine is as ridiculous as saying a woman is a little bit pregnant. Government rules and regulations, as well as Medicaid and Medicare, are socialistic.

So for some capitalistic (profit making) participants in our American health care system to claim we do not want a socialistic, 100 percent government-run health care system is pure *self interest bull*. The truth of the matter is our current health care system is socialistic and capitalistic. They mix like *oil and water,* which, as we all know, don't mix at all.

President Obama means well; however, our current health care system is beyond repair. It takes care of our senior citizens, our welfare recipients, our illegal immigrants, our emergency accidents and drive-by shootings, etc.

BUT WHO PAYS THE BILLS?

Two-thirds of all the babies born in America today are the newborns of illegal immigrants and welfare parents. We, the taxpayers, pay the astronomical costs of bringing a baby into this world under our so-called private health care system.

I AM SORRY, BUT WE CAN'T AFFORD OUR CURRENT SYSTEM

I am closing this article with two letters to the editor. One is from a doctor advocating a single payer system and one is from an elderly Canadian couple who defend their 100 percent socialistic, government-run health care system.

Single payer only way to save U.S. health care

To the Editors:

While I greatly respect both former Sen. Bill Bradley and Vice President Al Gore, neither of their health plans take into account what we know about how to achieve universal coverage at an affordable price.

What makes our system so expensive is we pay out 30 percent of our funds to cover the overhead expenses generated by the multiple insurance companies that administer HMOs. We know from our neighbors to the north this figure can be reduced to 10 percent with a single payer system that cuts out all the middle men.

By using a single payer system, Canada has been able to insure all its citizens at a cost that is less than what we are paying for a system that leaves 40 million people without insurance. Furthermore, their system allows consumers free choice of provider and physicians to decide what is "medically necessary" rather than some bureaucrat.

Why is it we keep coming up with these expensive and inadequate schemes when a cheaper and better model exists right next door? Is it because the insurance companies are poised with millions of dollars ready to put out another "Harry and Louise" media blitz of misinformation? You draw your own conclusions.

Dr. R.W. Chamberlin, Canterbury

Defending Canadian health care

I have just finished reading a letter (Beware Socialized Care, Letters, March 9) regarding an opinion on our health care system in Canada, and I take offense. I am a Canadian, as is my husband, and we have had quality care by the Canadian health system for more than 69 years. Between us we have had an appendectomy, gall bladder surgery, Achilles tendon repair, eye surgery, two knee replacements, bowel surgery with five days in intensive care, ankle surgery and numerous other ailments not requiring hospital care. All occasions were handled promptly and excellently.

Yes, for elective surgery, there would be a wait time. *This is good.*

If it's elective, it's not an emergency. For all the above mentioned problems, as well as our regular family health care, we have not had to pay any extra for anything. It is covered by our health care system, which we have paid for over years of taxes. We have a good system, and it should be considered a model for the USA – not criticized by persons who do not know what they are talking about.

A few weeks ago we visited a local hospital here in Florida for shingles treatment, and after about five minutes of conversation with a very pleasant doctor, we had to pay more than $700, which we did but considered it a lesson: We could fly home to Canada for treatment next time for less.

Karen Pipes, Hudson

If the current American health care system was a vehicle in an accident, it would be a total wreck. It is beyond repair, so I am suggesting we adopt the Canadian health care system. It's all we can afford.

13

WELFARE A STANDARD OF LIVING

Published 6/14/03

Whereas NH is currently working to meet the federal goals of welfare-to-work, and whereas a 20-year-old woman in the South is expecting her *third* set of twins while on welfare, I am asking *The Rochester Times* and *Foster's* to publish my view on the current welfare system.

I did pay for this column at my own expense, but now that I am retired I can't afford it.

I thank you for your consideration.

(This is a repeat of a political column I wrote on Aug. 6, 2001.)

What prompted me to write this column is a newspaper editorial from *The American Press,* Lake Charles, La. I have, at my own expense, reprinted this editorial which was in the Sunday, July 15 *Foster's.*

What other papers have said; no quick fix for welfare

It seemed so simple. Get work or get off welfare. Congress passed the law, President Clinton signed it ... Three years after the most comprehensive welfare reform in U.S. history, the structure is threatening to fall apart.

We're learning that it may take as long to solve a major social problem as it did for that problem to develop. That's a revelation politicians don't want to hear in an era of quick fixes designed to get instant voter approval.

Family heads who found jobs – on threat of losing welfare payments – are having just as much trouble paying for food, rent and utilities as those who remained on the welfare rolls, according to a national survey.

And ordering people to go to work doesn't mean it will happen. The survey of families either on welfare or just departed from welfare shows that major obstacles face people with little education or work skills when they apply for a job.

They either get no jobs at all or they get the lowest-paid, most menial jobs. And the majority of those menial jobs are the kind that don't allow for growth or development of skills. ...

What we've got is a welfare reform program designed to produce immediate success aimed at a problem in which expectations of immediate success are totally unrealistic.

Poverty, illiteracy and social disadvantages were generations in the making. It will probably take generations to erase those disadvantages.

The kind of education that will lift people out of poverty takes years to acquire for the first generation alone, and it takes another 16 years for the second generation to follow in the footsteps of the first.

It can be done – with time, patience and a lasting sense of responsibility.

American Press

Lake Charles, La.

THE GET WORK OR GET OFF WELFARE BILL PASSED BY CONGRESS THREE YEARS AGO WAS DESTINED FOR FAILURE

Three years ago when this comprehensive welfare reform bill as passed I wrote letters and told everyone who would listen to me that this bill would not work.

There are two major reasons why this new three-year *major* welfare reform bill did not work. The *first* is that it did not apply *any real incentives* for a person or family to get off welfare and join the workforce at a minimum wage with no health care benefits.

The *unsecured* wages that a welfare recipient would receive *for working* compared with the *secured* welfare payments plus welfare benefits they would lose provided no incentive for a welfare recipient to get a job and get off welfare.

There has got to be a greater difference in what Americans get *for working* as opposed to what welfare gives them for *not working*.

I think the national minimum wage should be increased by at least $3 per hour and that America's lower income (working poor) *should* be given the same health and dental care benefits provided to welfare recipients.

The second reason the three-year welfare reform bill did not work is ...

The American welfare system is *breeding* welfare families in America. Like it or not, realize it or not, welfare in America has become a standard of living for many American poor families.

In many cases the secured welfare income and benefits are better than the unsecured income of the working poor with no benefits. It's little wonder why *many* children brought into this world in a welfare family will at child bearing ages become the household head of a *new welfare family.*

THE WELFARE SYSTEM NEEDS TO CHANGE

I believe it is *not only* the moral obligation of a mother and father to *love* their newborn *baby but* it is also *their duty* to *provide* for that baby. So as of January of 2003 *no new babies* can be *added to the welfare* rolls.

If the mother and father, or the mother and *her* immediate family, cannot provide for their newborn they must surrender it to a *state or federal* run orphanage.

This orphanage for newborns whose parents cannot provide for them could be minimally staffed and maximum staffed with senior citizen volunteers.

In this orphanage the baby *in most cases* will get better care than it would get by being added to the welfare ranks.

Is an orphanage cruel and unusual punishment for a newborn baby? I don't think so. Most of the babies born into welfare have two *strikes* against them and society has three strikes against them.

The mother and father and immediate family who *cannot provide* for their newborn will have to *temporarily* put *the newborn* into a state-run orphanage. *They can visit their baby* on a daily basis. The new mother and father *can take* their newborn from the orphanage *when* they can prove they can provide for them.

I don't feel there will be many newborns surrendered to the state-run orphanages; however, we must have a place for the baby *if* the new mother and father *cannot provide for it.*

WE MUST STOP BREEDING WELFARE FAMILIES

If a current welfare family *cannot* get a new baby *added on the welfare rolls* and if an unwed teenage mother *cannot start a new welfare family* then the number on welfare is sure to *shrink year after year.* Why should welfare families continue to have babies and *why* should their teenagers create new welfare families when many working families wait to have a family until they can afford it *or* have one or two children because they can't afford any more?

I lived in Rochester, NH when I wrote about *true* welfare reform and my solution which was similar to this letter. A Rochester resident, "Diane Sharkey," chastised me for my proposal of taking a baby away from its mother and *placing* it in an orphanage. This was *her opinion,* which is fine, but *she* said I owned variety stores and *probably* gave my customers beer and cigarettes for food stamps.

I didn't comment on Ms. Sharkey's letter then, *however,* I do *not now* or *ever have been authorized to accept food stamps.* I never did apply for them because I know food stamp recipients can get more for the food stamps at the supermarkets.

ANYHOW, I AM GOING TO SEND THIS COLUMN TO *THE AMERICAN PRESS* IN LAKE CHARLES, LA.

Their solution, like many other intellectuals, is *better education for all will eventually wipe out poverty in America.*

I believe that better education will help *some* get off welfare but the welfare system needs a major *overhauling* if we are going to get the majority of American families off welfare and join America's lower income *(working poor).*

14

OPEN LETTER TO THE CALIFORNIA GOVERNOR

Published 1/21/10

Dear Governor Schwarzenegger:

Several weeks ago it was reported in the news media that you were going to Washington to request a $7 billion "bailout" from the federal government.

I assume you got it because California is "Too big to fail." You should have asked the President for a printing machine to print money like the U.S. government has because unless California makes drastic changes which allow them to balance their fiscal year budgets and start to pay down their debt, it will need $10 billion more next year.

We have, as of this writing, six big world-wide banks that are "Too big to fail". These big CEOs, drawing millions of dollars for themselves, have privatized their risky investment earnings while socializing their losses, leaving the U.S. taxpayer holding the bag.

These big banks (and they may be right) assume that the systemic risk of one of them failing would trigger a panic and cripple the whole American financial system.

There are other businesses – GM, Chrysler, AIG, Fannie Mae and Freddie Mac, the airlines, etc. – who use this "Too big to fail" argument to get U.S. taxpayers to bail them out. Most of these businesses have CEOs and board members drawing large salaries, with great benefits and pensions, while their companies are losing billions of dollars.

This is not how the free enterprise system in America is supposed to work. Those big banks and businesses who literally blackmail the American government for billions in bailout money because they are "Too big to fail" must and will stop because the American taxpayer hasn't got the money or the credit needed for the U.S. government to borrow trillions to bail out any more "Too big to fail" institutions and businesses.

Now comes California, the first of many states coming to the U.S.

government for a $7 billion bailout and getting it because they are "Too big to fail." When will this end?

The answer, Governor, is when California, the U.S. government and the other 49 states start to balance their budgets, live within their means, and start paying off our massive debts. If we don't do this, America will not be able to sell their treasury bonds and treasury notes. Then we will have to print more money with nothing to back it up.

Under this scenario, in the year 2012, we will have runaway inflation, with the U.S. dollar near junk bond status.

So, Gov. Schwarzenegger, I want to volunteer as a speech writer and, of course, you – being a former actor – can deliver this speech to the people of California.

> "To the citizens of California: I feel this speech is necessary for you to realize the gravity of our financial crisis in the State of California, our country, and all of the other 49 states in America.

> "We cannot keep doing business as usual. We have great fiscal problems in California which must be addressed or this socialistic cancer will continue to increase our state deficits, increase taxes, destroy the incentive to work, and increase unemployment.

> "The State of California must balance our new fiscal year budget and live within our means. We must not default on the interest California owes its bond holders.

> "We must stop subsidizing higher education in California, which we have done for decades now. We must stop breeding welfare families, as more and more of their children start new welfare families. We must change the laws because we have made welfare a standard of living with no incentives for those on welfare to seek work with low pay and no guaranteed benefits.

> "We must stop the U.S. government from letting illegal immigrants flood California. The ever-increasing number of illegals drives down the pay scale of poor and lower income workers. So while big business gets a cheap labor force, we, the State of California, have to subsidize these illegals for their education and health care costs. Not to mention the added police and prisons needed to stop the crimes committed by some illegal immigrants.

"So, fellow Californians, we taxpayers can no longer subsidize an ever-increasing welfare system and ever-increasing number of illegal immigrants coming into California. The welfare and illegal immigrant problems must be addressed before we can achieve a balanced budget. It won't be easy, but it must be done.

"Also, California, like all of the 50 states, is losing jobs to unfair so-called free world trade. All 50 states must demand fair world trade agreements and must bring back jobs to America in the manufacturing and technology industries.

"California must not raise taxes because, as President Reagan said three decades ago, 'A government big enough give you everything you want is big enough to take everything you've got.'

"So, my fellow Californians, I have laid out the problems which must be addressed before we become a welfare state with an economy equal to a Third World country.

"We, the businesses and taxpayers of this great State of California, must join together to cure California's socialistic cancer, which, if allowed to continue unabated, will destroy the state we once knew."

P.S. Also, when you meet with the businesses (large and small) in California and the taxpayers, ask them to vote against the new health care bill. This is an unfunded mandate which small and large businesses cannot afford. It is a socialistic boondoggle incognito. It will cause greater unemployment in California and in America.

I have many specific suggestions to help contain and lessen the growing welfare and illegal immigrant problems plaguing California. I would be glad to share them with you.

15

RISK IS NEEDED IN THE FREE ENTERPRISE SYSTEM

Published 12/20/07

I would like to republish my Aug. 9 letter to the editor.

2005 bankruptcy law must be repealed

The free enterprise system is so simple. You invest money into a business to get a return on your investment. This is called a *profit.*

However, in the free enterprise system there is always the *risk* of losing money on your investment. Take away the *risk* and the free enterprise system changes from allowing investors the *opportunity* to make a profit and becomes a *guarantee* to make a profit.

The credit card companies are businesses which issue credit to just about anyone, regardless of the *risk.* They render late charge fees of about 20 percent. They force many Americans into personal bankruptcy.

Up until 2005, a person who declared Chapter 7 personal bankruptcy could write off his or her credit card debt. That's the way it should be. However, in 2005 the credit card companies and their lobbyists got the U.S. Congress to pass the Bankruptcy Abuse Prevention and Consumer Protection Act of 2005.

This 2005 bill takes away the *risks* of the banking institutions who issue credit cards. The banks are secured creditors in a bankruptcy, which means a person declaring bankruptcy must still be liable for the full amount of his or her credit card debt.

We must amend or repeal the Bankruptcy Abuse Prevention and Consumer Protection Act of 2005.

When banks can no longer follow credit card debtors to the grave, they will think twice before they force debtors into bankruptcy with outrageous practices and charges.

In 2005, I wrote letters to the editor saying that the U.S. Congress should not pass this new 2005 bankruptcy bill, as it took the *risk* away from the credit card companies and that was violating the rules of America's free enterprise system.

The biggest secret now being held back from the American public is large banks and credit card issuers are carrying the $900 billion plus of credit card default on the balance sheets as *assets.*

The truth of the matter is these assets cannot be sold or borrowed upon. So in essence, these assets are really liabilities. That's why banks and credit card issuers are trying to extort money from any credit card holder to finance the bad debt credit card money on their books. Serves them right for trying to screw with the free enterprise system. Risk is needed to have the free enterprise system function correctly. Take away the risk and we have the malfunction result of $900 billion on the balance sheet of big banks and credit card issuers.

In case any reader can't correlate the heading of this letter, "You can't get blood out a turnip" means no way can the banks collect this $900 billion bad debt from the credit card holders who the credit card companies gave this $900 billion credit to. Why? They haven't got it.

16

A 'DEAR JOHN' LETTER TO MY FRIEND JOHN NOLAN, EDITOR OF *THE ROCHESTER TIMES*

Published 4/3/10

Dear John:

I would like to comment on your headline story last week, "Local Banks Concerned by Brewing Federal Regulation." Believe me; they have every right to be concerned. It's apparent that our U.S. Congress (which is controlled by big business) is, under the Federal Financial Regulatory Reform Bill, about to bury America's 8,200 small and medium size banks with a ton of rules and regulations that will restrict their independent, prudent business decisions.

As you stated in your story last week, our 8,200 American banks are not the problem of the U.S. and global financial difficulties which have our entire financial system on the verge of bankruptcy.

At the root of these seemingly unsolvable world-wide financial problems is their inability to solve the "too big to fail" problem with world-wide banks and financial institutions which poses a systemic risk to not only America's 8,200 domestic financial systems but the world's financial systems.

Not only can the world financial systems solve the problem of "too big to fail," they, with their lack of transparency, can't even recognize the big world-wide banks who caused this "too big to fail" financial crisis.

In my 2007 book *National Politics is Everybody's Business*, I have a chapter on "The 2005 Bankruptcy Law" and a follow-up chapter on "You Can't Get Blood Out Of A Turnip."

In these two chapters, I tell how the 2005 bankruptcy law took away the risks of the lenders (credit card companies and banks). When this 2005 bankruptcy law took effect in 2006 it gave the lenders a green light in regards to the consumer credit they were issuing. The lenders gave way too much consumer credit to too many Americans who could not pay it back.

So in 2006 and 2007 consumer deficit spending skyrocketed, along with federal deficit spending, leaving us with a false economy which was not sustainable.

In my chapter about the 2005 bankruptcy bill I said that "free enterprise is simple" – you invest to make a profit, and this is called a return on your investment. However, the free enterprise system has risks involved, and one could lose their investment.

So with the 2005 bankruptcy bill, the people and businesses who had to file for bankruptcy could not write off their credit card debt. This sand in the gears of the free enterprise system gave the credit card companies and bank lenders a guaranteed investment in issuing too much credit to too many bad risks. Since 2005's bankruptcy bill was enacted, the free enterprise system has been malfunctioning.

Now to make matters even worse, these large world-wide "too big to fail" banks sold most of their bad, uncollectable consumer debt, neatly packaged with real estate mortgages, to foreign banks and countries. They, under Triple A bond rating, sold Iceland so much bad, uncollectable collateral that it bankrupted the entire country.

Make no mistake about it, these large world-wide banks and institutions on Wall Street left the 8,200 American banking systems as well as the whole world banking system teetering on world financial collapse.

The second chapter in my book is entitled "You Can't Get Blood Out Of A Turnip." Simply said, the credit card companies and big banks carried $900 billion plus of bad consumer debt on their books as assets, but they were inactive, uncollectable liabilities. That's why Citi Group Inc. has no transparency in their balance sheets. They want to keep recent the inactive, uncollectable consumer debt they still have on their books.

So as the 2005 bankruptcy law gave the lenders, big banks and institutions the right to chase credit card debtors to their graves, they didn't realize you can't get blood out of a turnip, which means you can't get many one- and two-year delinquent credit card debtors to pay their indebtedness because they simply don't have it.

So John, these 8,200 American banks are the victims of the world-wide financial crisis and the Financial Regulatory Reform Bill is not needed to hinder the American banking system, which is already under strict government transparency and has their deposits insured by FDIC protection, which has worked for 70 years.

As you know, John, I have been writing columns for eight years or more under the headline of *National Politics is Everybody's Business.* I feel that the unfair new rules and regulations placed on America's 8,200 banks, the unfair advantages given to credit unions, and the newly proposed 22,000 government employees to provide us consumers with a Consumer Financial Protection Agency (CFPA) are all nails in the coffin of our financial system.

As Dear Abby used to say, "If it isn't broke, don't fix it." I say our 8,200 American financial system isn't broken, and more government rules and regulations will bury it, not fix it.

Now I am throwing out a challenge to all Rochester citizens. Get involved – because national politics is everybody's business. We should unite with the NH banking system and march on Washington. I will be in front of the group carrying a sign that says, "Don't dump on us. We didn't create the world-wide financial crisis" or "Americans who want to preserve our financially sound banking system."

17

GDP A FALSE ECONOMIC INDICATOR

Published 2/1/07

Our government and the media tell us Americans that our economy is good and strong. The basis of this assumption is that the GDP (Gross Domestic Product) has grown an average of 3 to 4 percent each quarter for several years.

True, the GDP has grown; however, the GDP is not a measure of prosperity nor well-being of the American people. In a good economy, most all Americans should be able to make ends meet and even save some money.

Today, in this false economy, more and more Americans are getting deeper and deeper in debt and cannot save any money. Also, our federal government in this so-called good economy cannot balance the budget. (In 2005, the deficit was $319 billion, plus the Social Security surplus of $175 billion equals a $494 billion deficit. America paid $327 billion in interest in 2005.)

Whereas the GDP measures all monetary transactions in the American economy, not all money accounted for in the GDP is good for the American economy and certainly not good for the majority of Americans who are not rich or poor.

So if the GDP goes up 3-1/2 percent the first quarter after the Katrina hurricane and many other negative things push the GDP up, how can an increase in the GDP be the barometer for calling the American economy strong?

In this commentary, I am not suggesting that the GDP figures are not helpful in measuring the strength of our economy; I am only trying to say that there is a better way to determine whether we truly have a strong economy or not.

I say we have a strong economy when the majority of us Americans (not the 10 percent higher income or the 30 percent lower income and poor) can pay all our taxes, purchase cars and homes, and not need any of the government taxpayer programs to make their living.

So when the majority of us Americans can pay our taxes, purchase high ticket goods and services and do not use any government (taxpayer) money, we are *assets* to a good economy in which the federal government should balance their budget.

So now that we know that Americans who pay their taxes, purchase goods and services, and do not need help from the government are assets to the economy, who are the liabilities?

When our federal government tells us they have created over 7.2 million new jobs, what they don't say is that the great majority of these jobs are liabilities to our economy. These jobs pay so little that these 7.2 million new employees pay little or no taxes, purchase no high ticket goods and services, and use every taxpayer government program that is available to the American poor and the illegal immigrants as well.

So as the assets to the American economy get few and fewer and the liabilities get higher and higher, America's true economy gets weaker and weaker.

Instead of using the GDP as a measuring stick for our economy, we should get quarterly reports of the number of American workers who are assets to our economy. If we can maintain or grow our assets then the economy will be a true economy, not one built on increasing consumer debt and increasing federal deficits.

If America continues to lose good paying jobs (assets) and increases low paying jobs (liabilities), our American economy will get weaker and weaker, even if the GDP grows and grows.

18

THE IRS MUST BE REPLACED

Published 4/27/10

The IRS is not producing the revenues needed to grow our economy. The fact that more poor and lower income Americans pay little or no taxes and the rich and big business have tax loopholes, plus the growing number of Americans who don't even file any income taxes, compiled with many tax cheaters – it's little wonder why federal revenues are declining when they should be increasing.

We also have a growing underground economy in America as more and more Americans and illegals are dealing with cash only and not paying any income taxes. This underground economy is at least $500 billion a year.

We must have a national consumption tax (aka national volume added or national sales tax) as of Jan. 1, 2011. We can make it 10 percent on everything. Five percent of this national consumption tax goes to the federal government and five percent goes to the states to pay for the unfunded mandates the federal government passes.

Also, as of 2011, the IRS should cut IRS taxes in half and make them much more simple.

In a year or two, if the national consumer tax increases federal and state revenues, we can double it to 20 percent and nearly eliminate the IRS.

A national value added sales tax will let America receive revenues from goods sold in America by slave labor countries and eliminate the cash-only underground economy.

Whereas I suggest that the states receive 50 percent of the revenue received by a national sales tax (aka value added tax) the states could collect and monitor this tax. With the exception of two or three states with no sales tax, they could implement and enforce this consumption tax with a few new employees.

19

MAKES SENSE TO ME

Published 10/18/07

There is a growing movement in America to replace the IRS and all other federal taxes with a 23 percent federal sales tax. This consumption tax is called the Fair Tax and is explained from A to Z in Neal Boortz and John Linder's best selling book, *The Fair Tax Book*.

In my opinion, the 23 percent federal sales tax (consumption tax) is the only way to get the large corporations (American in name only) to pay their fair share of taxes to the U.S. government.

As it is now, these large multi-national corporations are investing in Third World countries like Vietnam, where they work for much less than $1 an hour. This manufactured product made in Vietnam is shipped to America and sold for the highest price possible. The final result is (like trade with China) Americans losing good jobs in our country.

Now I ask anybody: How can America compete with slave wages like that? The answer is that we can't. So as America loses more good jobs each year from "free world trade," the American government receives *less* federal taxes as the large corporations in America lay off workers with good jobs year after year.

In the last Republican debate, Fred Thompson was asked about the state of the American economy. Fred said, "The American economy is strong and is experiencing 22 quarters of increased GDP (Gross Domestic Product)" etc., etc.

I have a follow-up question for Fred. How come in the last 22 quarters (nearly six years) the federal deficit has risen from $4.8 trillion to over $9 trillion?

The answer is that America has a false economy buoyed by federal deficit spending and consumer deficit spending. It is an unsustainable economy which will not have a soft landing when the bubble bursts.

The IRS is not providing the money the U.S. government needs to balance their budget. The Fair Tax has a name which implies that we are swapping the IRS for the Fair Tax because it is fair to the American people. This is not the reason. The reason is that the IRS, in this era of unbridled globalism, is not getting enough taxes to supply the American government with their fair share of taxes in the global marketplace.

With the new consumption tax (called Fair Tax), the U.S. will get 23 percent of all goods sold in America regardless of if they are made in China or Vietnam.

Also, the Fair Tax will make all the underground economy (which is billions and billions) pay their taxes (which they currently don't pay a penny of) and the people profiting from the sale of drugs will also pay taxes when they purchase their new home or Mercedes automobile.

Yes, getting rid of the IRS for a 23 percent consumption tax is the number one issue in 2008. If our government doesn't have the money it needs, how can the U.S. government continue to operate without experiencing a financial crisis?

So I cannot support any candidate for president in either party (or possibly third party) who does not want to get rid of the IRS for a 23 percent consumption tax (Fair Tax).

20

OUR *REPUBLIC* IS LONG GONE; OUR *DEMOCRACY* IS DEAD – WE JUST HAVEN'T HAVE THE *FUNERAL* YET

Previously Published

When Benjamin Franklin came out of the office with the signed Declaration of Independence, he was asked, "What do we have here?" Ben replied, "We have a *republic*, if you can keep it."

Well, we all know we couldn't keep our *republic*, that's why we no longer recite the Pledge of Allegiance to the American Flag and the *republic* for which it stands, etc., etc.

When Al Gore was running for President in 2000, his wife, Tipper Gore, gave a speech at the University of New Hampshire in which she quoted Ben Franklin *incorrectly*. She quoted Ben as saying "You have a *democracy*, if you can keep it."

I wrote a letter to the editor and I said, "Tipper, Tipper, Tipper. Ben Franklin said 'You have a *republic,* if you can keep it,' *not* 'a *democracy,* if you can keep it.'"

Well, our *republic* is long gone and Tipper's *misinformation* of "You have a *democracy,* if you can keep it" is *true* as could be.

While most of us Americans celebrated our 233rd July 4th Independence Day with cookouts, Boston Pops concerts and fireworks, I was, in *my own mind,* attending the *wake* for our *democracy,* which will have its funeral the end of 2009 – that's this year, folks.

If *independence* and *democracy* go together like love and marriage "go together like a horse and carriage," and they do, then you can't have one without the other.

Globalization has taken away our *national sovereignty* and our right to control our own economic destiny. When we became a *dependent* nation instead of an *independent* nation, we lost our *democracy.*

It's not only the large world-wide corporations – whose goal is manufacturing goods at the lowest labor costs worldwide, selling as high as possible in the American marketplace and paying as little taxes (with their loopholes) as possible – that *promote globalism.*

It was three major events which put sand in the gears of America's free enterprise system, which provided the majority of us Americans the opportunity to work hard and better our standard of living.

The first was LBJ (1964-68) and his socialistic Great Society programs, which were pushed then by the Liberal Democrats. The second was the $6 trillion federal deficit given to us by Bush and his *so-called* Conservative Republicans. And the third was we, the American people, who voted for politicians who are going to give us everything we want while not raising our taxes. This is what changed America from the land of opportunity to the land of guarantee, thus killing our *democracy.*

LBJ'S GREAT SOCIETY SOCIALISTIC PROGRAMS
1964-68 FOR OUR AFFLUENT SOCIETY

One of John F. Kennedy's famous lines in his 1960 presidential campaign was, "Ask not what your country can do for you, but what you can do for your country."

I guess LBJ and the rest of us Americans didn't pay any attention to JFK's famous political proclamation.

Let's see, it's now 40 years (1969-2009) since the socialistic foundation of Great Society programs and we now have a welfare society. More poverty than 1969, more people who can't get health care than 1969, more who can't afford college without student loans than 1969, and many more senior citizens being cared for by the taxpayers than 1969.

I guess I am different from most Americans. I figure my parents gave up so many material things for us, their children, that – *with a few exceptions* – we should take care of our parents when they get to old age.

Part of the problem with our health care system (not all of it) is that we seniors are using up too much of the resources in the health care system.

They say future growth in our economy will come from the health care and education system and, of course, government jobs. It's too bad the average American cannot afford health care or a college education.

ENTER 2000 TO 2008 WITH GEORGE B.A. BUSH AND HIS $6 TRILLION (DEFICITS DON'T MATTER) TWO TERMS. IN MY MIND, BUSH'S MIDDLE INITIALS SHOULD HAVE STOOD FOR BENEDICT ARNOLD.

Of course, President Ronald Reagan, 1980-88, spoke like a Conservative Republican; however, he was the grandfather of deficit spending. Karl Rove, who was George W. Bush's political advisor, told George *deficits don't matter.* Don't raise taxes and just blame the Democrats for the deficits. Karl Rove and George Bush pushed America into *insolvency.*

When I hear Conservative Republicans like Senator Judd Gregg say Obama will bankrupt the country, I say that he can't do that, Bush has already bankrupted the country.

One thing President Reagan said is truer than ever today. He said, "A government big enough to give you everything you want is big enough to take everything you've got."

Bush's last budget will end on Sept. 30th of this year with a true deficit of $1 trillion. Obama's $3.5 trillion budget begins Oct. 1st of this year. He acknowledges that this astronomical $3.5 trillion will carry a $1.8 trillion deficit. This is based on 2 percent growth of our economy, which will not happen. Obama's 2009/2010 budget deficit will be well over $2 trillion.

America, having lost our *republic years ago,* will lose our *democracy* the end of this year. We will have a recession and depression at the same time, which will lead to socialism because of our country's fiscal irresponsibility.

As America becomes socialistic in 2010 we will have to help millions of unemployed Americans put food on the table and provide government housing for the homeless.

Then, of course, we will need a 10 percent national sales tax, which will cause a tax revolt throughout America.

How can we have a recession and depression at the same time? Well, people who are not in debt, have a good job and/or savings will be in a recession while getting taxed to death and the Americans who are unemployed will need government programs to put food on the table and a roof over their heads.

Yes, it will be a *recession* when your neighbor's out of work but it will be a *depression* if you're unemployed.

IN MY BOOK, *NATIONAL POLITICS IS EVERYBODY'S BUSINESS,* I OFFER MANY SOLUTIONS TO AMERICA'S GRAVE PROBLEMS.

Concerned Americans must accept reality and offer constructive criticism to our government, even if nobody listens to you.

21

DEMOCRATS AND REPUBLICANS HAVE FAILED

Published 11/24/09

The Democratic and Republican parties are not looking out for the best interests of America and the American people.

I personally was very displeased with George W. and the Republican Party. I registered and voted Democratic in 2008 and am now very displeased with the Democratic Party.

It seems both parties are controlled by the large world-wide corporations and put the world economy first and the American economy second. It's bad enough the large corporations give millions of dollars to both the Democratic and Republican parties; we have another very *disturbing* factor happening on the national political scene – that is the extreme liberal left trying to take over the Democratic Party and the extreme conservative right trying to take over the Republican Party.

The extreme left and the extreme right are fighting each other while the American economy is losing jobs to a rigged game called free world trade.

The unemployment rate is 10.2 percent, with another 7 percent unemployed but not collecting benefits. This is really 17 percent unemployment in America, and it could very well be over 20 percent in true unemployment by the end of 2010.

So while the extreme left and the extreme right in America are blaming each other for our unsustainable economy, which needs $2 billion a day of borrowed money to finance our deficit spending, our country is heading toward bankruptcy.

So what we need in America is a true third party to represent the best interests of the American people. What name for this party could possibly be better than the Nationalist Party? It could be comprised of Independents, moderate Democrats (yes, there are still some Democrats who are not in the liberal left) and of course, Republicans who have no answers to today's complex global problems and realize their party doesn't have any answers to these problems other than cut spending and cut taxes.

Yes, this new Nationalist Party will have more in numbers than the Democratic and Republican Party together. They will be a force that will truly represent America *first* and the world *second.*

There is an old saying: A dog can't have two masters – and we must make Obama and the new president-elect in 2012 know that we are their masters, not the G-20.

So some would say we already have the option to register as an Independent. Registering as an Independent just shows that you are not pleased with either the Democratic or Republican Party. It does not give you any clout in the ballot box, where you have to vote for either the Democratic or Republican candidate for President of the United States. Many Independents know that a vote for any other presidential candidate would be a wasted vote as their choice could not win. So they are, as the old saying goes, voting for the lesser of two evils.

If we had a strong Nationalist Party made up of Independents, *conservative Democrats* and *moderate Republicans*, we could take America back.

We can, through great political upheaval, *regain* our national sovereignty and control our economic destiny. These goals must be accomplished if we want to take America back from the economic disaster which globalization is leading us into.

Lee Iacocca wrote a book a few years ago asking "Where are the leaders in America today?" I would like to replace that question with "Where are the followers today?"

Would the average American follow a national leader for president in the new Nationalist Party? I think not. Most Americans are like the weather – we all complain about it but it seems nobody does anything about it. Well, we obviously can't do anything about the weather but complain. However, we could follow the leader of a new third party in America – the Nationalist Party.

Yes, a leader could step forward, but it would take an army of followers to break up America's two-party system, which allows the Republicans to blame the Democrats and the Democrats to blame the Republicans, while it is apparent both parties are to blame.

22

ONLY AMERICA PRACTICES FREE TRADE

Published 12/31/09

One of the many words of wisdom my mother taught me was to "take things from whom they come."

In 2003, then-millionaire entrepreneur (now billionaire) Wilbur E. Ross stated on the front page of the *USA Today* newspaper: "The World Trade Organization (WTO) is a wealth transfer organization not in the best interests of America, and the problem with free world trade is that only America practices it."

The man who made this public statement in 2003 was not a politician, not a college professor, not an economist, and not a spokesman for the large, world-wide corporations or any other so-called business expert who never sold a can of beans or met a payroll in their lifetime. This profound statement on the WTO was made by a participant in global trade.

So when Wilbur E. Ross says, "The World Trade Organization (WTO) is a wealth transfer organization not in the best interests of America, and the problem with free world trade is that only America practices it," I remember what my mother taught me, to "take things from whom they come."

If we are going to get our jobs back in America we must get new fair trade agreements with every one of our trading partners. We first must get out of the WTO and try to regain our national sovereignty if we are going to control our own economic destiny. It's probably too late; however, if we don't get our jobs back from an unfair global marketplace we will be taxed to death to pay for our socialistic system.

We lost our republic under the Hoover administration, 1928-32; we entered our democratic system under Franklin D. Roosevelt in 1932; and we are being escorted into a new socialistic system under Obama in 2009.

Make no mistake about it; we have entered the socialistic system of government.

Whereas we did not vote for socialism – it was forced upon us due to our federal government's fiscal irresponsibility – we will have great protests and violence in every big city in America.

I was drafted into the U.S. Army Infantry, November 1952 to November 1954. Since 1964's LBJ administration, I have been fighting the growth of socialism in America. We didn't get socialized overnight, and we will not get de-socialized overnight. We Americans must halt the growth of socialism and roll it back by balancing our federal budget and paying back our deficits, which we can't do unless we get the jobs back in our own economy which were taken away from us unfairly.

Forced socialism, if enforced by the National Guard or federal troops, is called communism.

23

THE HOUSING CRISIS

Published 7/26/07

In the past few years I have written several letters to the editor in regards to the ever-rising prices of homes (new and old). They were very over-valued and I couldn't see how middle income families could afford the mortgage payments and NH's highest-in-the-nation property taxes.

I was especially concerned about the new homeowners in NH who not only carried a $200,000 or $300,000 mortgage and still pay NH property taxes on their over-valued and over-appraised home. I knew that what goes up must come down, and the so-called mortgage meltdown is only the tip of the iceberg.

Mortgage meltdown

The meltdown of the subprime mortgage market was as predictable as the morning sunrise or the swallows' return to San Juan Capistrano. Borrowers' financial ignorance, combined with lender greed, has undermined both our financial institutions and the real estate economy.

An unholy alliance of predatory lenders and unethical realtors and appraisers has led to phony appraisals and doctored loan applications. It has devastated the financial lives of many borrowers, it has defrauded financial and real estate investors, and it has jeopardized numerous businesses that service the real estate sector.

As Yogi Berra so aptly put it, "It ain't over 'til it's over." The subprime meltdown will now reverberate through the prime real estate market. Home values will continue to flatten, and those homeowners who are facing fat loan balloons, or have used their home equity as their personal cash cow, will stare into the abyss. This is more than a few rotten apples. It is systemic fraud.

When will it hit bottom and what will the bottom be? A well known economist predicted 2009 and home values 30 percent less than today's home prices.

If he is correct, a $450,000 home today will be $315,000; a $300,000 home will be $210,000; a $200,000 home will be $140,000; and a $100,000 starter home or condo would be $70,000. This bottom of the mortgage meltdown will be in the next two years.

Yes, 2009 is right around the corner, and I have two suggestions for NH homeowners. Write your NH Congressman and Governor and tell them, "I am fighting foreclosure on my home and NH should start doing the math, substituting the NH property tax for an 8 percent sales tax." This 8 percent sales tax will equal the 8 percent room and meals tax we already have.

A personal friend of mine said, "Well, if property values go down, we NH homeowners will pay less taxes." *Not so,* whereas in NH we have no income or sales tax, if our property values go down they will just raise the tax evaluation.

So if your NH property tax evaluation goes down, your tax rate will go up.

The second piece of advice I have is if you're selling your house now, lower the asking price and accept any reasonable offer from an interested, qualified buyer. Your house will be worth 30 percent less in two years.

Also, if you have a house with three or four bedrooms and several baths, look for a person to rent a room and bath from you. Because if a husband and wife get divorced, or have huge hospital bills, or one loses their job, chances are you will get backed up financially and face foreclosure.

Last but not least, when the housing prices hit bottom, many homeowners will not have enough equity in their mortgage because their $300,000 home is now worth $210,000. Believe it or not, lenders can issue foreclosures to homeowners who have not missed a mortgage payment. They simply say "because of property devaluations we must have $20,000, $30,000 or $50,000 more on your mortgage or we will foreclose."

We should write our U.S. Congressman today and have them pass a law which will not let the lenders foreclose on any up-to-date loans because the home is worth less due to the real estate market. The way our U.S. Congress moves, we need to act now.

24

AMERICA'S SPUTTERING ECONOMIC ENGINE

Published 1/8/10

Here is how so-called free world trade is unfairly taking away American jobs.

America was the engine that the world economy depended upon for growth in their private sector. Foreign governments, friend and foe alike, knew that by taking good jobs in manufacturing and technology from America and them exporting those goods to the American marketplace was a proper way to grow.

Our trading partners' governments did not grow their economies by extending their consumer credit beyond the ability of their workers to pay the accumulated debt back, nor did they simply let their government engage in deficit spending far above their ability to pay it back.

It's too bad America did not have the business sense to realize the consumer deficit spending and federal deficit spending would produce a false economy which, at some time, would have to be paid back.

As they say in business, "Growth without profits is false growth." An economy without a balanced budget is a false economy, as a family's standard of living is a false standard of living if they are living way beyond their means.

Foreign governments, (our trading partners) with the exception of the U.K., have not followed the American government's reckless deficit spending and not let their citizens create huge consumer debt.

As the old Wall Street firm of Smith-Barney used to say, "We make our money the old fashioned way, we earn it." I haven't heard that slogan for years now.

Not only did the U.S. government create a false economy with their consumer and government deficit spending, they – with their laissez-faire policy of unbridled globalism – let those large ("too big to fail") banks sell underfunded collateral and grossly over-leveraged American assets to anyone in the world stupid enough to buy these overvalued assets.

I guess in this letter I have put the carriage before the horse. I now want to backtrack and tell you how America's so-called free world trade should have been implemented.

First of all, America should never have given up our national sovereignty (which is needed to control our own economic destiny). We have lost our sovereignty to the WTO and to the G20 world economic organization.

Secondly, we should have segregated our trading partners into two groups. The first group would be the industrialized countries who have similar pay and benefit scales, environmental laws and a freely elected government. To this group we should have stated we would open our American markets to them 100 percent; however, they must open their markets to American exports 100 percent.

Also, our industrial trading partners must not manipulate the value of their currency to increase their exports to America while decreasing America's imports to them. They must not put tariffs on American goods going into their country and must stop subsidizing their countries' businesses to allow them to sell cheaper in the American marketplace. This practice is called dumping.

Any industrialized nation who is not abiding by reciprocal free trade agreements will face immediate retaliation in our free trade agreement. America can no longer let industrialized foreign countries bend and break our free world laws.

Now that we have laid down the law to our industrial trading partners, we must put tariffs on countries that employ slave labor and pay wages of $1 to $2 an hour. How can American workers compete with slave labor countries without gradually losing jobs year after year?

I know the argument for letting slave labor goods into America is we get lower prices and this keeps inflation down. Yes, this is good, as one reason for inflation is "too much money chasing too few goods and services." However, letting slave labor goods into America without any tariffs also has brought consequences which are not good for the American economy and the American way of life as we know it.

First, slave labor goods put Americans out of jobs; second, they drive down the lower and middle income American workers' salaries and benefits;

and this practice also pours oil on the socialistic system, which America has now entered.

Make no mistake about it, when American workers don't get paid a living wage and cannot put food on the table or pay their rent or mortgage, then the federal government must subsidize them and, of course, raise taxes on all other Americans.

There is another big problem that I have with slave labor goods flowing freely into the American marketplace with no tariffs: Wal-Mart receives 90 percent of the goods that China ships to America. Wal-Mart is a monopoly and endangers America's domestic competitiveness. I know, and in another article I will make my case against Wal-Mart.

They are cut-throat competitors who target existing businesses and successfully eliminate domestic competition. They are not unionized (and they should be) – they are now nationwide, going after America's large supermarket chains.

Kroger, America's largest food chain, pays union wages and benefits. They lost $750 million their last fiscal year. This was because of Wal-Mart.

Just think – if Wal-Mart can control the food industry, what next?

Well, how about them taking slave labor manufactured goods, buying them for $6.00 and selling them with no competition for $19.00?

It's ironic how the Federal Trade Commission (FTC) is suing America's Intel Corporation because of reported monopolistic pricing in the world marketplace when Wal-Mart, who is a world-wide corporation, is fast eliminating all their domestic competitors with unfair, cut-throat pricing.

In a future letter, which will probably be longer than this one, I will give you my experience with Wal-Mart's cut-throat competition.

25

SOCIAL SECURITY PAYS ITS OWN WAY

Published 2/7/08

In the early 1970s, the U.S. government came up with a good piece of legislation. Knowing that the Social Security Trust Fund would need much more money to pay out to the baby boomers, they made employers match the 6.2 percent withdrawn from their employees' paychecks on a weekly basis.

So for many years now the Social Security system has paid 12.4 percent each paycheck to the Social Security Trust Fund. When the employers had to match the employees' 6.2 percent payroll withholding tax, it doubled the money paid in to Social Security.

Add to this the decade of the '70s with 100 percent inflation rate wages, and Social Security payments to the U.S. government skyrocketed.

In 1983, the Republican administration transferred the Social Security Trust Fund into the general government revenues. Since 1983 (with the exception of the Democratic Clinton administration of 1992 to 2000) the federal government has been using the Social Security Trust Fund as a cash cow. They have taken over $3 trillion from the Social Security account.

The highly respected Concord Coalition speculates that Social Security will be in red ink by the year 2017. When that time comes, (sooner or later) the U.S. government can do a few minor adjustments to make sure the Social Security system is alive and well.

Social Security is one of the few government programs that pays for itself. It may have a slight cold in 2017 but it will need only a teaspoon of cough syrup to ensure its recovery.

However, it is the health care system entitlements which will bankrupt the U.S. Each year, health care costs in the U.S. go up about 10 percent more. It serves fewer and fewer Americans at higher and higher costs. Unlike Social Security, it is not funded by the 12.4 percent withholding tax.

For politicians to put Social Security in the same unfunded entitlements as health care is a big lie. Social Security may have an adjustment in 2017;

however, the health care entitlements will bankrupt the U.S. Treasury in 2010.

In 2005, the financial report of the United States says the U.S. federal deficit was $318.5 billion plus $175 billion taken from the Social Security Trust Fund.

So the true federal deficit in 2005 was not $319 billion but $494 billion. I don't mind the U.S. government spending the Social Security surplus to lessen their true budget deficits; however, I detest the fact that they haven't leveled with the American people that since 1983 the government has spent $3 trillion of Social Security money.

The federal budget is in near bankruptcy; the health care system is an entitlement which will put a few nails in the coffin of the federal budget. However, the Social Security system is well financed and can meet its obligations in the future.

Don't let politicians tell you how they are going to fix the Social Security system. Social Security is the last thing that needs fixing.

26

THEY DON'T HAVE A CLUE HOW
TO GET OUR JOBS BACK

Published 12/10/09

I suppose if we rule out all the ways our federal government is trying to create jobs for American citizens in our own economy, just maybe they can insist on fair world trade to bring back American jobs.

First of all, our government is trying to spend their way out of this deep-rooted recession with deficit spending. This is an effort in futility, as it was consumer and federal deficit spending which were the main reasons for our unsustainable economy in the first place.

Any public sector jobs created by our federal government will be temporary employment. True job growth must be created by the private sector. So rule out federal deficit spending, aka stimulus deficit spending, as a jump-start to America's economic battery. You can't jump-start a dead battery.

Now as for our government and CNBC Wall Street analysts telling us the consumer's holiday purchases are going to pull the country out of our recession – that's ridiculous. Consumer spending may be two-thirds of our economy, however, two-thirds of today's consumers are in debt or living paycheck to paycheck.

So we ruled out federal deficit spending and consumer spending to spur our economy, creating permanent jobs, what's the next false ray of hope? It is that small business alone will provide new jobs to our economy. As a small businessman all my life, let me tell you unequivocally that small business, under current market conditions, will not create new jobs and will lose jobs is 2010, 2011, 2012, etc.

Small business needs the consumers to receive good paychecks so they can pay their taxes and have money left to purchase goods and services provided by small business. It has been documented that for every manufacturing job, three other small business jobs are created.

So for job creation, we have ruled out federal deficit spending, aka stimulus packages, consumer spending and small business. What's next to rule out? How about ruling out the fact that consumers and small businesses in particular cannot borrow money in today's credit crunch?

The fact of the matter is few consumers and few small businesses have good enough collateral to get bank loans. Banks will not make bad loans just to create jobs for our economy.

Let's see now; we have ruled out federal deficit spending, consumer spending and a tight credit market – what's the next unworkable method to create jobs?

How about the false assumption that cutting taxes for those with higher incomes (the rich) and yes, big business, will create investment in the American economy and create permanent jobs? Well, that isn't the way the free enterprise system works. You can cut taxes to virtually nothing, however, if the recipient of these tax cuts does not have the confidence that an investment into the American economy will give them a return on their investment, (a profit) that's what stops them from investing in the American economy.

Believe me, if there was a buck to be made by investing in the American economy, private sector money would be plentiful. Call it capitalism or greed, that's what spurs investment, which in turn creates jobs.

Tax cuts for the rich or for big business is a sham. They will take their tax cuts and invest in China.

There are many other ways to rule out accomplishing job creation, but I can't leave out higher education. For our government and many other intellectuals to give our kids the hope that a college education will ensure them a six-figure job upon graduation is a false assumption; the truth of the matter is over 50 percent of the graduating college students in 2010 will not be able to get a good job, which they will need to pay off their student loans.

Nothing could be worse than graduating from college with no job and a $40,000 student loan to pay off.

The U.S. government today is putting students in debt which three-quarters of them cannot pay back – much like putting Americans into homeownership which, with greedy lenders, led us to the sub-prime housing crash.

By 2011 we will have a student loan default which will be larger than the sub-prime housing debacle.

This letter is already too long; however, I would like to offer some constructive criticism on our inability to provide good jobs for our college grads in 2010, 2011, 2012, 2013, etc.

The bottom line is we must demand fair world trade, even if it starts a job and trade war. We must bargain for jobs from a position of strength. Our strength is our $14 trillion economy.

Let the world-wide economic war begin.

27

IT WAS STILL ABOUT JOBS IN 2001

Published 9/6/01

The Federal Reserve board has given us seven interest rate cuts in the last year or so in an effort to create the SPARK which would fuel up the engine of the American economy.

The last ¼ percent interest rate cut DROPPED the stock market over 100 points on the day it was announced.

Although the battery which propelled our economy to nearly a decade of economic growth was probably a DIE-HARD BATTERY, it is now DEAD.

The American economy doesn't need any more "jump start" interest rate cuts, WE NEED A NEW BATTERY.

HOW TO FIX THE AMERICAN ECONOMY

We create NEW JOBS in all sectors of America's PRIVATE SECTOR. Our economy today is TOO DEPENDENT ON PUBLIC SECTOR JOBS. The two growth industries in America are jobs in health care and education. Both those public sector industries provide jobs with taxpayers' money.

To call a spade a spade, both health care and education ARE SOCIALISTIC. Both will need more and more taxpayers' money in the years to come.

Health care and higher education have become TOO EXPENSIVE for most Americans to pay for by themselves.

DECREASE PUBLIC SECTOR JOBS AND INCREASE PRIVATE SECTOR JOBS

That's the key that WILL JUMP START our economy. Further interest rate cuts WILL NOT HELP.

How did our American economy become (as we are today) SO DEPENDENT on public sector jobs? Or should I rephrase the question and ask WHERE did all our private sector jobs go?

We can blame UNFAIR free world trade (which is controlled by world-wide corporations) for our loss of domestic jobs in our PRIVATE SECTOR.

Most everything we USE or WEAR in America is made in a foreign country.

I guess there was a SHORT TERM advantage of flooding our American market with foreign goods which took away millions of jobs in our private sector.

The short term advantage was that these tons of foreign goods in our American marketplace HELD DOWN INFLATION for the past 10 years. I guess this simplistic reason for inflation is TOO MUCH MONEY chasing TOO FEW GOODS AND SERVICES.

There has been little or no inflation in the American economy for the past 10 years, NOT ONLY because of foreign goods flooding America's marketplace but because the American consumer HAS NOT GOT TOO MUCH MONEY.

I have to LAUGH when I hear over the news media that America's CONSUMER SPENDING (which accounts for 2/3 of our economy) may pull us out of a RECESSION or conversely if CONSUMER CONFIDENCE is down and they don't spend then we will have a PROLONGED RECESSION.

THE TRUTH OF THE MATTER IS

The majority of average American consumers are head over heels in debt. However, the American consumer will KEEP SPENDING as long as credit is EXTENDED to them and they can buy big ticket items with LITTLE or NO down payment.

The majority of American consumers will CONTINUE to BUY NOW and PAY LATER. So CONSUMER SPENDING and CONSUMER CONFIDENCE has little to do with HOW we replace the DEAD BATTERY which has driven our economy to a standstill.

My next week's political column will provide suggestions of how we can return America's free enterprise system BACK TO the PRIVATE SECTOR.

28

THE TRUTH ABOUT VISAS

Published 5/24/03

We the American people must demand FAIR WORLD TRADE to replace UNFAIR free world trade. In order to adopt a new FAIR world trade policy we must resign (GET OUT) of the WTO (World Trade Organization) immediately if not sooner.

This is the #1 issue in the 2004 presidential campaign.

I am reprinting this letter.

Visa program gives American jobs to aliens

To the Editor:
Most Americans have never heard of theH-1B visa program. But a growing number of high-tech engineers, programmers and electronics specialists have found out about it the hard way.

In 1990, Congress and President Bush (the elder) created the program, which allows variously skilled foreigners to enter the United States. In the year 2000 alone, 355,605 arrived and accepted lower pay for jobs that were taken away from Americans. Since the program began, between 800,000 and 1 million jobs have been lost to foreign workers. Ask someone who has been replaced by a foreigner with a "temporary" H-1B visa and you'll discover that it's not temporary.

H-1B isn't the only program some firms are using to reduce their payrolls with foreign workers. Companies possessing an overseas division can funnel workers hired outside our country into jobs here in the United States with L-1 visas, another program favoring outsiders over Americans. There were 294,658 L-1 visas granted in the year 2000.

Congress should be told to abolish both the H-1B and L-1 visa programs, not only to keep jobs of Americans from being taken by non-citizens but to maintain America's leadership as a first world power.

William McNally
Windham

29

HOW THE WTO TRANSFERS WEALTH

Published 9/20/07

About five years ago, then millionaire (now billionaire) Wilbur E. Ross made a public statement that I haven't heard repeated since.

He said (and I still have the front page *USA Today* article), "The World Trade Organization is a Wealth Transfer Organization not in the *best interests* of America, and the *problem* with free world trade is that only America *practices* it."

When I ran for President of the U.S. in the 2004 Republican primary, my main issue was fair trade. So quite naturally I demanded that the U.S. get out of the WTO. In the 2004 primary, *only* Democrat Dennis Kucinich *was then* and *still is* today demanding the U.S. get out of the WTO.

WHAT IS WEALTH? AND HOW IS IT TRANSFERRED?

The wealth of a nation is all the workers who have good jobs. They pay the most taxes, purchase the most goods and services, and don't use any of the taxpayers' money to subsidize their standard of living.

That's the *wealth* of a nation. The more good jobs a country provides for its workers, the *wealthier* the country becomes. Conversely, the more good jobs it loses, part of its *wealth* goes along with the job losses.

So that's how the WTO transfers *wealth* from America around the world with *unfair trade agreements* that do not benefit the United States of America but benefit the large world-wide corporations in their quest to buy as cheap as they can world-wide, to sell as high as they can world-wide, and to pay as little taxes as possible world-wide.

RIGAZIO FOR PRESIDENT 2004

Did I really have any political aspirations of becoming President of the U.S.? *Of course not.* However, I was very serious about my solutions to the many problems in 2004 that have now become near crises.

I received a little more than 1,000 votes in the 2004 Republican primary election. Myself and two others got about 1,000 votes each and George W. got 53,000 votes.

I figured *if* I could have gotten 5,000 or 6,000 votes the media would pay attention to my campaign issues. It didn't happen. I also figured the public who *disapproved* of George W. Bush's policies would have given me some protest votes; it didn't happen.

Well, what did it cost me? Besides the $1,000 fee to be on the NH ballot, I spent nearly $200,000 of my own money. I sent back five checks totaling $200 to someone who wanted to help my campaign. I had a first-class website and spent most of my money in newspaper ads in *Foster's* and *Manchester Union Leader.*

Knowing what I know now, would I still have run for President in the 2004 NH state primaries? *Hell no.* For Americans to re-elect Bush shows how uninformed we are on national issues.

It's just poetic justice that Bush got re-elected so he can be in office when his war still divides the country and his federal deficits will cost us $400 billion a year in interest each and every year, and he leaves our economy in a very bad recession due to his economic policies.

God bless America and the new President of 2009 and the American people who will be paying for George W. Bush's eight years in office for years to come.

After reading this column, I would be less than honest if I didn't say what bothered me most about my running for President in 2004 was the people who viewed my candidacy as a big joke and didn't even read my positions on the issues.

And to my immediate family who felt I was embarrassing them: To this I tell them publicly, T.S.

30

THE EARTH IS NOT FLAT; SMOOT HARTLEY TARIFFS DID NOT CAUSE THE FIRST DEPRESSION

Published 10/22/09

America's economy is losing good jobs every year because of unfair trade.

Whenever I and other common-sense American citizens call for fair trade, we get branded as protectionists.

Although our economy is heading toward becoming a third world nation economy and we have lost our democracy, which is going to be replaced by a socialistic government, we still have politicians, college professors, economists and other intellectuals crying about how fair trade is going to rekindle the Smoot Hartley flames.

All these educated Americans who blame the American depression in the early 1930s on the Smoot Hartley legislation, which imposed tariffs on foreign goods, are like people of yesteryear who insisted that the world was flat.

Our depression of the early 1930s was caused by manipulation of a skyrocketing stock market and the greed of the American people who thought they could borrow money to invest in the stock market, which was in reality a Ponzi scheme.

The stock market collapsed in the first depression because it was grossly over-leveraged, not because of the Smoot Hartley legislation.

What irks me the most about these yesteryear statisticians − who call any legislation to achieve fair trade protectionism and warn of the Smoot Hartley bill causing the depression − is their greed.

Then I got to thinking about these politicians, professors, economists and CNBC/Wall Street experts who say every piece of legislation which will insure America's fair trade is a protectionist act and then recite the Smoot Hartley bill. They are all alike.

Do you know what they all have in common? They will not lose their jobs in this rigged game called free world trade. Their jobs will not be outsourced.

These people who have job security and low prices because of no tariffs are the same self-interest groups who are against any taxes.

I classify them as "self-interest, deficits-don't-matter conservative republicans" who look at the world economy first and the American economy second. They will soon realize that deficits do matter and we must have a strong economy if we want to keep the family values that we all cherish.

My father had only two family values. First was "Provide for yourself and your family" and second was "Obey the laws of the land."

Pretty soon, we protectionists will have nothing left to protect

First, I am reprinting Richard Driscoll's letter to the editor, 8/19/03.

Conned into giving our jobs and nation away

To the Editors: We have been conned into giving away our nation. No nation has ever maintained its standard of living or a prominent position in the world once it has lost its industrial base.

The United States is rapidly losing its industrial base, it is losing its manufacturing jobs, it is losing its high-tech jobs, and it is losing its ability to be self-sufficient, all with the blessings of both political parties. Not one candidate for the office of President of the United States has stated that if elected he would stop this hemorrhaging of American Jobs to overseas locations.

Richard Driscoll, Plaistow

I would like to reprint this 8/11/07 letter to the editor.

Loss of white-collar jobs hurts millions

First they came for the blue-collar jobs. I didn't care, because I had a white-collar position ("USA's new money-saving export: White-collar jobs," Cover story, Money, Tuesday).

Then they came for the computer and engineering jobs. I didn't say a word, because I had an office job. Now they're coming for my job, and there's no one left with a job to speak up.

Oh well, such is the cost of free trade.

Now, can someone please tell me how I and the millions of other displaced American workers are supposed to make our livings, raise our families, pay our mortgages and other housing expenses and send our kids to college?

I expect I will have to wait for an answer to that question until the party of the free traders and the unregulated marketplace is deservedly swept out of power.

John Woodmaska, Kearny, N.J.

Do any of you "free world traders" have an answer for Mr. Driscoll or Mr. Woodmaska? If so, I would like to hear from you.

31

THE INFLATIONARY '70s

Published 3/31/08

I am writing in reference to your March 10 editorial, "No quick fix is on the way." The subheading on this editorial was "Bernanke may soon have to say stop stagflation."

To set the record straight, we did not experience stagflation in the decade of the 1970s. What we had in the '70s was inflation caused by the power of the big labor unions to demand and receive wages and benefits that far exceeded their productivity. Big business simply applied follow-the-leader price increases, causing inflation.

Whereas the standard definition for inflation is too much money chasing too few goods and services, the inflation of the 1970s was caused by labor and big business. How did the big labor unions and the big businesses get into this envious position where big labor could receive wage and benefit increases each year and big business could make profits by simply raising prices?

Well, we have to go back to 1968, where LBJ let the airline industry receive a 19 percent wage and benefits contract. Until that time, JFK had the Kennedy wage and price guidelines in effect. Big labor could not navigate any contract exceeding 6 percent per year and big business could not raise prices more than 6 percent per year.

During his time in office, Kennedy and his successor, LBJ, held big labor and big business within the 6 percent Kennedy guidelines. The business world was watching LBJ who, with his jawboning power and the withholding of government contracts, could have stopped the 19 percent airlines contract which broke the 6 percent Kennedy wage and price guidelines. LBJ, because of 1968 congressional elections, chose to do the politically popular thing, which was to let the airlines' union break the Kennedy 6 percent wage and benefit guidelines.

So, what started out as a wage and benefit inflation became a price and wage inflation as big business raised their prices before uncovering wage union contracts. This resulted in yearly inflation rates of 10 percent or more and 100 percent inflation for the decade of the 1970s.

Needless to say, we had to stop inflation. They had to raise interest rates to 10 percent or more each year in the 1970s, so whereas big business did not have to invest money to increase productivity, they simply made profits by raising prices. The decade of the 1970s was not stagflation. It was inflation caused by big business and big labor.

The only similarity between the 1970s and today is that many middle and lower income Americans, whose wages and benefits are not keeping pace with inflation, cannot purchase as many goods and services or pay as much taxes.

In the decade of the 1970s the inflationary cost of living went up equally for all Americans; however, the wages and benefits of many non-union workers did not receive wage increases.

Americans were pushed into the lower income wage earners. Yes, the 1970s did much to decrease the number of Americans who are today called the middle class.

So in 2008, 2009 and 2010 we will not have stagflation or inflation. We will have a recession, which many will call a depression. Many Americans will not be able to put food on the table, gas in their gas tank and pay ever increasing state and federal taxes.

If you were a non-union worker in January 1970 and your wages were $200 a week, your wages and benefits (if you had any) must have risen to $400 per week on Jan. 1, 1980. The inflation rate for the decade was 100 percent, so the cost of living went up 100 percent for everyone. So if at the beginning of January 1970 your wages were $200 per week and on Jan. 1, 1980 your wages were $240 a week, your standard of living went down $60 per week.

So the decade of the 1970s did much to lower the standard of living for America's lower and middle income Americans.

Isn't it ironic that today the airlines who broke the 6 percent Kennedy wage and price guidelines want we the taxpayers to guarantee their pensions, which were between their labor unions and big business?

No way should the U.S. taxpayers guarantee their pensions.

32

HE PLANS ON DYING BROKE

Previously Published

I never wanted to be a millionaire; I just wanted to live like one. Just kidding. While people who know me and people who think they know me believe me to be rich, I am going to die broke.

I do have my financial security, providing I die in 2009. I never was one who, with their portfolios, tries to emulate Donald Trump and to invest their money to increase their net worth.

I do not have any stocks, bonds, 401Ks, pensions, savings accounts, etc.; I don't own any property. I do have a Social Security check and a checking account. I do have a weekly check 'til I die from the sale of my three variety stores several years ago, so I don't think I will be living under a bridge – although you never know.

Did I mention I don't own any stocks? Guess I did – just one of those senior moments, or as I like to say, I have a good memory but it's short.

Anyhow, about three or four years ago I was telling one of those Donald Trump wannabes that I never bought a stock in my life. I said I figured the stock market was manipulated – and speculated – with no transparency to the amount of derivatives, hedge funds, etc., and questioned the earning sheets of the companies in the stock market. So my friend said, "John, where do you put your money?" I said, "I have it invested in my businesses" – however, I am not a financial expert.

Just put your money where the principal is 100% safe and then try to get the best rate of interest you can get.

I can't believe pension fund money was and is invested in the risky stock market to gain higher interest rates. When the stock market crashes again, the smaller investors will lose their shirts while the big investors will have their money already out of the market.

I guess by now you know what I think of investing money in the stock market. However, I will say I would rather have Wal-Mart stock than U.S. Treasury notes.

With the money I have given away in past years I could be a millionaire, but that was not my goal. I will, in a couple of years, if I am lucky, die broke – and the last check I write will be to the undertaker (and make sure it bounces!). Just kidding.

Some say money isn't everything; although it is people with money that usually say that. Money can't buy everything; it can't buy poverty.

Remember that old saying, "It was love at first sight"? Today that is being replaced by the saying "It was love at second sight – the second time I saw him I knew he had money."

I am the biggest tipper in New Hampshire, probably New England. I feel that I am in the higher income bracket and most waitresses and waiters are in the lower income bracket and can use the extra money.

Upon receiving their tip, most waiters or waitresses say, "Are you sure?" Then, "Thank you, you made my day!" So why don't you people (who think you can take it with you) leave your waitress or waiter a big tip and make their day?

It's a long story, so I'll give you a *Reader's Digest* version of how anyone's financial status can change. After 20 years of running a large business, I went broke. I had very bad legal advice and lost everything I had.

However, I never lost my work ethics, and being lucky enough to be living in America, where you are never a failure until you stop trying, I made my financial comeback.

I worked in a furniture store and as an assistant manager at Sawyer Mills and Seigel's supermarkets. It was in Seigel's when I thought I was going crazy because I was talking to myself and I had no money in the bank. A very nice lady told me that she also talked to herself because she liked an intelligent conversation. I have never forgotten that.

So in April of 1985 I opened Signal Street Variety with $15,000 working capital. I worked 90 hours a week for the first two years and built a business doing $15 million a year.

There are takers and givers in this world. I am a giver because I feel so good when I help out others who, through no fault of their own, need help.

33

CAPITALISM IS NOT A FORM OF GOVERNMENT

Published 11/12/09

Michael Moore's new movie, "Capitalism: A Love Story," is entertaining and thought-provoking. However, it is total fiction.

Capitalism is not a form of government, but rather a formula which (if not tampered with) will give Americans the incentive to work long hours and invest in the economy to better their standard of living.

Capitalism is the byproduct of the free enterprise system; it is not a form of government and cannot be blamed for the economic hardships that many Americans are now experiencing.

So I would advise the critic of capitalism (Michael Moore) to take all of his huge profits made under our capitalistic system and divide them equally between all the poor and lower income Americans. If he does that, capitalism would indeed be a love story.

Ruling out capitalism as a form of government, there are, in our modern day history, (1900-2009) three forms of government.

First was a republic, second was a democracy, and third is a socialistic government. America has already entered this form of government.

Whereas we Americans did not vote for a socialistic system of government, it will create much taxpayer revolt in America. Now if we need the National Guard or government troops to quell this taxpayer revolt, then our socialistic system becomes a communist system.

Pretty scary, isn't it?

Now, as briefly as possible, I want to tell how we lost our republic and how we lost our democracy.

Herbert Hoover was a great American who was elected by a landslide in 1928 as President of the United States of America. Many Americans used their savings and even borrowed money to invest in the manipulated, ever-escalating stock market, and the crash of the stock market made many Americans penniless and without a job.

It was during his term (1928-1932) that Hoover did not realize the gravity of the situation. Because he wanted to abide by the Constitution and the republic for which it stands, he resisted using federal government money to assist businesses or help the growing number of poor people in America.

Yes, our republic was in Hoover's term, 1928-1932. He should have, as Roosevelt did in 1932 when he became President, entered into the new system called a democracy. Whereas America was in a world-wide depression, the government had to give the people hope and programs to pump money into our economy and take measures to render much needed security and confidence so the American people would again put their money in banks and invest in our American economy to create jobs.

Some Conservative Republicans today blame Roosevelt and his "New Deal" government intervention into our economy as the departure of the principles of our Constitution and the killing of the republic system. When Ben Franklin was asked about the Constitution, "What do we have here?" he replied, "You have a republic, if you can keep it."

You see, a republic was the system that gave the states their own authority to make their own laws and regulations. The federal government, under a republic, was supposed to maintain a military for defense of the country, to run the postal system, and possibly a few other things that states needed government control for.

Do I blame FDR and his "New Deal" for pounding the last nails in the coffin called our republic? Of course not. He did what he had to do to bring the country out of a depression. Now, some 70 year later, our democracy has died. We just haven't had the funeral yet.

What killed our democracy? Government fiscal irresponsibility and the American voters who elected politicians who proceeded to give them everything they wanted while not raising their taxes.

Of course, unfair trade and globalization have also played a great part in killing our democratic system.

I would like to come to the defense of Herbert Hoover, who was elected President in a landslide victory and lost his second term bid in a landslide loss. He was snubbed by FDR and was not recognized until Harry S. Truman asked him to accept a position as U.S. Ambassador to Europe, which he did. Hoover died in 1964.

Hoover did acknowledge that during his term in office, he should have deviated from the Constitution and abandoned the principles of the republic.

Hoover did sign the Smoot Hartley Bill during the depression, along with the majority of other congressmen. This bill put tariffs on foreign goods.

Economists at that time (I guess some should have been in the U.S. Congress) voted unanimously against the Smoot Hartley legislation and even went on to blame the U.S. depression on this legislation.

Well, let's talk business. If we hadn't passed the Smoot Hartley Bill, what would have happened? Well, if foreign countries exported tons of goods to America, who in the U.S. had the money to buy them? We in America provided a demand for goods but had no money to pay for the cheap exports to America.

The problem in the U.S. depression was not *inflation,* it was *deflation.*

So without the Smoot Hartley Bill, foreign exports to America would not have helped get us out of a depression but rather would have taken away a few of the jobs we needed so desperately in America.

Yes, we can blame Hoover for not putting federal money into the people's hand in the depression, but we cannot blame the Smoot Hartley legislation for causing the depression.

There is an old French saying, "The more things change, the more they stay the same." Well, one thing has changed today, and that is our federal government *not* putting money into our economy. That's when the socialistic system begins in 2010.

34

ABOUT SUPPLY AND DEMAND

Published 5/10/07

In the free enterprise system, we are told that the price of a certain commodity is governed by the law of supply and demand. Oil is *supposedly* in short supply, and the demand is at an all-time high, thus we have high gas prices.

Well, I only went to high school but I can tell you that the law of supply and demand does not work when too few control the supply or too few control the demand. The fact that OPEC, which only contributes 17 percent of all the world's crude oil, can monopolistically control the supply leads me to ask: Where are the other 83 percent who control five times more crude oil than OPEC?

The answer is that the 83 percent are not competing in price for a portion of the world oil market but rather are playing follow-the-leader prices set by OPEC. As I mentioned earlier, the law of supply and demand doesn't work when too few control the supply or demand.

Not only does OPEC and the 83 percent of others control the crude oil but they, and the large oil companies, control the refineries which control the inventory of our refined gas and heating oil.

If that isn't enough monopolistic pricing powers, the large oil companies control the retail gas stations and engage in non-competitive retail price fixing at the gas stations. There are a few areas in America where there is still some competition in price; that's why prices in some states are lower than most of the other states.

So the law of supply and demand doesn't work when too few control the supply or the demand, which leads to no competition in the drilling, refining and retailing of crude oil.

The fact that our Congress and our President can say gas prices and heating oil prices are a result of free market supply and demand is beyond comprehension. They say if we decrease our demand that prices will fall.

No way will gas and oil prices go down if we in the U.S. decrease our demand. We are between a rock and a hard place. The rock is OPEC and the other 83 percent of the monopolistic cartel and the hard place is their partners – the big oil companies. Too few control the supply (OPEC) and too few control the wholesale and retail distribution of that supply.

Present gas prices and the prospect of higher gas prices will put the U.S. economy into *deflation* within a year. The American consumer will have little or no money to purchase other goods and services needed to sustain our economy, never mind grow our economy.

America must create competition for OPEC and the large oil companies. We must build, as soon as possible, five or six huge (non-profit) refineries. With our U.S. refineries building up our inventories, we will not face shortages or fear of shortages. We then could sell our refined gas to large national retail chains like Wal-Mart to bring competition in price to the retail section of the oil industry.

If America cannot free ourselves from the monopolistic pricing powers of OPEC and the large oil companies, we will not be able to control our own economic destiny.

Throughout this guest commentary I have stated that the laws of supply and demand don't work when too few control the supply or too few control the demand. Make no mistake about it, we in America, along with China, Japan and the European Community, do control the *demand*. By controlling the demand we can restore competition back into the crude oil industry.

Remember, they need our dollars as much as we need their oil.

If anyone has read this far in my commentary and come to the conclusion that America cannot build non-profit (government owned) refineries, I say we can't continue with our massive trade deficits, budget deficits, declining dollar, and the possibility of deflation or a recession in our American economy.

35

GLAD SOMEONE KNOWS
WHAT'S GOING ON

Previously Published

I read the daily newspapers and watch TV news programs. I consider myself pretty well informed on what's happening to America.

I was aware of the FAST TRACK legislation called Presidential Trade Promotion Authority. However, I DID NOT READ ANYWHERE in the media WHAT this piece of legislation MEANT to America and to our ability to control our own ECONOMIC DESTINY in the near future.

I am, at MY OWN EXPENSE, reprinting Margaret's letter to the editor for ALL AMERICANS to read, so they may call their congressmen to VOTE NO on the Presidential Trade Promotion Authority. Let's DERAIL this FAST TRACK legislation, which is in the best interests of the WTO (World Trade Organization) and NOT IN THE BEST INTERESTS OF AMERICA AND THE AMERICAN PEOPLE.

TO THE EDITOR

In the midst of our national grief, many fail to recognize the threat to our democracy explained by the following letter:

By stealthy and clever tactics, a coup is under way that can deal a body blow to our democracy. The coup is in the form of a trade agreement that will supersede present U.S. law and become law for every country in the Americas, except Cuba. It is wrapped in rosy promises of dedication to democracy and a better life for all, and has an innocuous-sounding title, "Free Trade Area of the Americas" (FTAA).

The rosy promises have no teeth, but the essence of the agreement has very sharp teeth. The essence includes a startling reversal of the right of government to regulate business for the benefit of the public. Over the years our government, through democratically passed laws, ended child labor, established the 40-hour week, assured a safe food supply, and much more. To enforce those laws, government could fine businesses.

The FTAA turns things upside down. Corporations can sue governments for passing any law that would be a barrier to their present or potential future profits. Suits will be settled, not by the courts, but by three-person tribunals meeting in secret. The value of a law for the well-being of people or the environment is irrelevant to the tribunal. Judgment is based solely on how much profit would be lost. Fines can be sufficiently huge to force governments to rescind laws.

So much for government of, by, and for the people.

The giant corporations leading this coup know that an informed public would not support it, so they want Congress to approve the FTAA by a special "fast track" legislative process that would eliminate public hearings with expert testimony, prohibit amendments, and limit debate.

The vote on "fast track" (now called "Presidential Trade Promotion Authority") may come soon. Please ask Smith, Gregg, Bass and Sununu to oppose "fast track" and uphold the right and duty of Congress to hold public hearings, consider amendments and allow thorough debate.

Margaret Tillinghast and others
Durham

AGAIN, THANK YOU MARGARET

What I would like to know is what OUR NH CONGRESSMEN think about the Free Trade Area of the Americas (FTAA) and the fast track Presidential Trade Promotion Authority???

If our NH Congressional leaders DO NOT INFORM their CONSTITUENTS (NH citizens) about FTAA and the Presidential Trade Authority we SHOULD vote them OUT OF OFFICE IN 2002 AND 2004.

36

ECONOMY GOING BUST

Published 10/29/09

There are two real dark clouds hovering over the American economy. One is the future of the U.S. dollar and the other is the pending Chapter 11 bankruptcy of Citi Group Inc. (too big to fail?).

Several years ago, 50 economists were asked what they feared most about the problems facing the U.S. economy. All 50 said the American dollar going into freefall.

With the current administration adding trillions to the national deficit and printing more U.S. dollars with nothing to back it up, we could see the American dollar in freefall within one to two years.

What is holding our U.S. dollar up is our $14 trillion economy. Foreign countries hold about $6 trillion in U.S. treasury bonds. These trading partners are no longer buying U.S. treasury notes. If it was not for their favorable trade with America they would cash in the treasury bonds they are holding.

This would be the worst case scenario, as the U.S. is now having problems selling U.S. treasury bonds and treasury notes.

We need to put Americans back to work and start balancing our federal budget.

The systemic risks the Citi Bank (now called Citi Group Inc.) Chapter 11 bankruptcy will have on our U.S. financial system are frightening.

If Citi Group Inc. can orchestrate a panic-free Chapter 11 bankruptcy it will be because they are too big to fail. I just hope the U.S. taxpayers don't bear the brunt of Citi's financial restructuring.

We already gave billions in taxpayers' money to G.M. so they can build G.M. cars in China. When will our President and U.S. Congress look out for American jobs in this rigged game called free world trade?

37

DEFICITS MUST BE PAID FOR

Published 4/30/07

People are only interested in the small part of the economic puzzle which affects them immediately and directly.

The Republican Party, since Reagan, Bush Sr. and George W. Bush, have told the public what they want to hear, plus they not only pledge no new taxes but they, under George W. in particular, are in the process of huge tax cuts.

So, Americans, wake up. There is no free lunch. If we as a nation do not balance our budget, we will keep raising our national debt and increase the interest we have to pay on the deficits.

In the 2005 fiscal year, we paid $327 billion in interest, and in the fiscal year of 2006 we paid $360 billion in interest, mostly to foreign countries.

So the Republicans say the Democrats will raise your taxes if elected, but they continue to increase our national debt and increase our yearly interest payments.

In my opinion, the Republican administration under George W. Bush is like a CEO and we the American people are the shareholders. He is borrowing $2 billion a day and pledging the assets of we the American people as collateral.

Yes, folks, deficits do matter and the only difference between increased taxes and interest payments on our national debt is that the tax increases are the small part of the economic puzzle which we Americans are concerned with.

38

AMERICA IS CAUGHT IN A 'FREE TRADE' TRAP

Published 12/3/09

When our government ends its fiscal year Sept. 30, 2010, I would like the following information.

First of all, I would like the trade imbalance with every one of our trading partners in dollars. We can start with China, Japan, India, South Korea, Canada, Mexico, Germany, France, Vietnam, etc., etc.

Now I know this request is just a matter of record and can, within a month, be made public. What isn't made public is the number and quality of the jobs our imports from all our trading partners takes away from our American economy and how many jobs our exports to the same countries provides for our American economy.

Giving us figures, in dollars, of our trade imbalance just tells us where our money has gone. For example, (and these are ballpark figures) if China exported $380 billion to America and they only imported $90 billion from us, they had a $290 billion trade imbalance with America.

Now what I want to know is how many *jobs* did our exports to China give us and how many jobs did our imports from China take away from us?

We should get these job imbalance figures from every country we do business with. Naturally, many of the small, poor and developing countries will not take away a significant amount of jobs from our economy; however, all job imbalance figures must be monitored – the same as the dollars are monitored.

What these job imbalance figures will show is what I already know – all of our trading partners are shipping us goods that provide jobs for their citizens and are only importing from us commodities plus other goods and technology they need to grow their economies.

So, under the false premise of free world trade, our trading partners are taking away jobs that should belong to the American economy.

I don't get out much anymore; however, if you do see an old man with gray hair and a blue face, that's me. I have been repeating myself 'til I am blue in the face.

I have said this for nearly seven years now – what then millionaire (now billionaire) Wilbur E. Ross said on the front page of the *USA Today* newspaper: "The World Trade Organization (WTO) is a wealth transfer organization not in the best interests of America, and the only problem with free world trade is that only America practices it."

It's little wonder to me how President Obama won the Nobel Peace Prize. Of course, what he didn't know then and still doesn't know now is there is an ongoing economic war, with every country (except America) fighting for jobs for their citizens.

So after every country asked Obama the same question – "Are you going to let America resort to protectionism?" – Obama, being naïve or uninformed, (whichever adjective you want to use) answered, "No, I don't believe in protectionism, I believe in free trade."

These foreign countries, being protectionists themselves, embraced Obama and were instrumental in awarding him a Nobel Peace Prize when he had been in office for only six months.

I guess they also were pleased that Obama had restrained Israel from bombing strategic nuclear facilities in Iran and publicly told Israel to stop any building in the West Bank, which Israel can't do without taking away a lot of their country's security.

Sooner or later, Israel, for their own existence, will have to take out (bomb) the nuclear facilities in Iran. It's going to be a lot harder for Israel to take out these nuclear facilities in Iran six months to a year from now than it would have been a year ago, before Obama won his Nobel Peace Prize.

Sticks and stones may break my bones but names will never hurt me. Call me a protectionist, but if we don't put America's citizens back to work in our own economy, we have no chance of an economic recovery.

The strength and stability of the American dollar and American financial system, while avoiding runaway inflation in three or four years, depends on putting Americans back to work. Our goal for total unemployment in America should be six percent by 2012.

39

WAKE UP AMERICANS: OUR ECONOMY IS DYING

Published 10/15/09 (Originally published 8/03)

FREE WORLD TRADE is nothing more than a BUNCH OF BULL-CRAP. Whereas ONLY AMERICA PRACTICES IT, we ARE SUBJECT TO UNFAIR WORLD TRADE AGREEMENTS WHICH ARE KILLING OUR ECONOMY.

We must pass AMERICAN LAWS in our Congress (immediately if not sooner) to STABILIZE and REBUILD OUR MANUFACTURING JOBS. We also must pass laws to SAVE OUR HI-TECH INDUSTRY.

In order to SAVE THE AMERICAN ECONOMY, we must GET OUT OF THE WTO (World Trade Organization).

A year and a half ago the United States PROVED that foreign countries were DUMPING STEEL in the U.S. MARKETPLACE for WAY BELOW COSTS and that THEIR COUNTRIES' GOVERNMENTS WERE SUBSIDIZING THEIR LOSSES.

AMERICA PLACED TARIFFS ON THOSE FOREIGN STEEL COMPANIES and STEEL IMPORTS TO THE U.S. HAVE GONE WAY DOWN in the last year and our DOMESTIC STEEL INDUSTRY HAS STABILIZED AND INDEED IS GROWING.

On JULY 12TH the WTO (an unelected body) ruled OUR TARIFFS on FOREIGN STEEL ILLEGAL. In the WTO, AMERICA HAS ONE VOTE along with every other country who has one vote. America IS TAKING OFF OUR TARIFFS (20 percent this coming year and completely the year after).

What is the matter with the President, the U.S. Congress, and we the American people for letting the WTO DECLARE AMERICAN LAWS ILLEGAL?

As Wilbur Ross, a C.E.O. of a new U.S. steel company, stated in a recent speech, "The WTO is a WEALTH TRANSFER ORGANIZATION and is HOPELESSLY WEIGHTED AGAINST U.S. INTERESTS and the TRAGIC FLAW in FREE TRADE is THAT ONLY THE U.S. PRACTICES IT."

I would like to reprint this 8/11 letter to the editor

Loss of white-collar jobs hurts millions

First they came for the blue collar jobs. I didn't care, because I had a white-collar position ("USA's new money-saving export: White-collar jobs," Cover story, Money, Tuesday).

Then they came for the computer and engineering jobs. I didn't say a word, because I had an office job.

Now they're coming for my job, and there's no one left with a job to speak up.

Oh well, such is the cost of free trade.

Now, can someone please tell me how I and the millions of other displaced American workers are supposed to make our livings, raise our families, pay our mortgages and other housing expenses and send our kids to college?

I expect I will have to wait for an answer to that question until the party of the free traders and the unregulated marketplace is deservedly swept out of power.

John Woodmaska
Kearny, N.J.

Jobs jobs jobs

The 2004 Presidential Primary and the 2004 Presidential Election has ONE OVERRIDING ISSUE and that is RESTORING JOBS BACK TO AMERICA'S DYING ECONOMY.

40

HOW LONG CAN OBAMA HOLD BACK ISRAEL?

Published 10/4/07

America does not have to worry about Iran building nuclear weapons. Israel will not let that happen. With their intelligence, Israel will bomb any Iranian nuclear facility whenever they feel it's necessary. Why wouldn't they? Do you honestly believe Israel will let Iran develop nuclear weapons, which Iran will use to destroy Israel?

After Israel destroys all of Iran's nuclear facilities, will Iran start a full-scale war against Israel? Hell no, they fear Israel's military power! They will cry to the UN and other world powers.

Israel has its borders secure and they retaliate after every act of terrorism. Besides their battle proven military, Israel has a nuclear arsenal as a deterrent to any other country who would even think of destroying Israel.

One must remember – Islamic fanatics, with their uncivil acts of violence against innocent men, women and children, are cowards who run away from conventional war on the battlefield.

Just look at their six-day war against Israel 20-some years ago; just look how they ran away from battle in Desert Storm; look how they ran away from America's forces when we took Saddam Hussein out of power in Baghdad. Islamic militants only know terrorist war, they will not fight on the battlefield.

Why do you think Israel has survived all these years?

1. They have their borders secure.
2. They retaliate for every terrorist act upon their country.
3. They have a military super power ready to spring into action.
4. And last, but not least, they have nuclear weapons as a deterrent.

So to America I say: Don't worry about Iran having nuclear weapons, Israel will not let that happen.

Also, I want to warn the Iranian people: Be careful what your crazy, loudmouth Iranian president is wishing for – he just might get it.

The Iranian people must realize that pursuing nuclear weapons will bring total destruction to Iran. Forget nuclear weapons.

41

LET ISRAEL TAKE OUT IRANIAN NUCLEAR FACTIONS

Published 10/29/07

IRAN

The President of Iran, Mahmoud Ahmadinejad, several years ago publicly denied the Holocaust and promised to destroy Israel and America.

Since then, Iran has supplied terrorists with money, weapons, missiles, and roadside bombs to be used against America and Israel. They have let up on Israel after their failed missile assault launched from Syria a year or so ago.

Make no mistake about it; Iran fears retaliatory reactions from Israel, that's why they are holding back terrorist acts on Israel.

However, Iran, with Russia's backing, is pursuing nuclear weapons to destroy Israel. They simply will give terrorist groups the nuclear weapons to destroy Israel.

Iran, as of now, does not fear an attack on them from the United States because they know the U.S. Congress and the American people will not let this happen.

ISRAEL

Israel will not let Iran proceed with their plans for nuclear weapons. They, sooner or later, will have to launch all-out air strikes against Iran's nuclear facilities and military installations.

The Israeli people – whose mothers, fathers, grandparents, aunts and uncles, nieces and nephews, and friends were murdered in the first Holocaust – will not let a second Holocaust happen in their lifetime.

The fact that Iran has publicly announced the destruction of Israel and is hell-bent on securing nuclear weapons, plus the latest announcement by Iran that it has 11,000 missiles to be launched if Israel attacks them, is provocation enough for Israel to proceed with the inevitable war with Iran.

AMERICA

America must let Israel attack Iran alone. This cannot be a dual attack on Iran by Israel and America.

Now as soon as Israel's planes bomb Iran, Iran will launch some, or as many as possible, missiles at Israel.

If Iran sends any of these 11,000 missiles to American forces in Iraq, to any American war ships or American bases in the Middle East, then we can retaliate with our superior Air Force and Naval superiority and a real war will begin and end shortly.

The American Congress and the American people will not let Iran rain missiles down on Americans without full retaliation.

THE AFTERMATH

Once Israel and America have literally destroyed all of Iran's military capabilities, we can leave Iraq. The Iraqis don't want us there. They even said a few weeks ago that they don't even want U.S. bases in Iraq.

Yes, after we take care of Iran we can all come home and say mission accomplished!

The civil and religious battles in the Middle East will continue, with a group declaring itself the winner. However, Iran will not be able to pick up all the pieces and Iran's President, Mahmoud Ahmadinejad, is not going down in history as the Hitler of the Middle East who started World War III.

42

MAIN STREET USA REVIVING DOWNTOWN

Published 3/26/10

Can downtowns across the U.S. be the robust shopping places that town and city residents used to *patronize*? The answer is yes and no. It can be done, but not without a game plan which will give the consumer value for their shrinking dollar.

PLAN A – SPECIALTY STORES

Get a good downtown location and specialize in fresh fruit and produce. Buy your fruit and produce directly from the Boston market. Two truckloads a week of fresh produce bought direct and sold at retail could give consumers overall lower fruit and vegetable prices than any supermarket.

This retail specialty shop could buy potatoes by the trailer load directly from Maine and sell them at below retail prices.

A fruit and produce market – like the one my father owned in the late '40s at 48 North Main St. – could work with people who have experience in the wholesale and retail produce business. Of course, this produce center could diversify, selling eggs, bread, beverages, etc., but sell all of these items below supermarket prices.

If I wasn't pushing 80, I would enjoy the challenge of opening a retail produce store on Main Street.

STILL PLAN #1

A retail meat specialty shop on Main Street, run by a working manager who knows his business, could do a good business in a good downtown location. Again, with exceptions to the supermarket weekly meat specials, a privately owned meat specialty store could undersell 80 percent of the retail meat prices below any supermarket.

COST + 10 PERCENT

Over 45 years ago, a man named Fred Hildreth came up with the concept of dry groceries for less than supermarket prices. As a wholesaler, I sold him many truckloads of groceries. When he retired, I rented his retail operation and successfully ran the *cost plus 10 percent* operation.

Fred's *cost plus 10 percent* was a concept where he priced most of his goods at or below his wholesale costs and simply added 10 percent to the total order. Like a specialty fruit and produce and/or specialty meat store on Main Street, the *cost plus 10 percent* concept will offer consumers lower prices on 80 percent of the supermarkets' overall prices.

However, it is a *volume business* that needs to do big business to lower operating costs.

THE FIRST NATIONAL, NOW THE EMPTY
HOFFMAN'S FURNITURE STORE

If a knowledgeable, experienced entrepreneur could rent the Hoffman storefront for $2,000 a month and run a *cost plus 10 percent* concept on 100 percent American made or American grown goods, they could bring in thousands of customers every week.

The concept is only 100 percent American made goods, sold at *cost plus 10 percent*. The signs and window posters for this new concept would be "Buy American – the job you save may be your own." The official name would be American Made Main Street Outlet Inc., "Most all goods marked at *cost plus 10 percent* added a checkout. We sell any and all American manufactured goods that we have room for. American quality at near slave labor prices."

Whereas the NH advantage is no income tax and no broad based sales taxes, this *cost plus 10 percent* will be very well accepted. If a customer's total purchases were $549 subtotaled plus 10 percent added would make the total $603.90.

Yes, NH's no income and no broad based sales tax is perfect for a *cost plus 10 percent* operation. We in NH might as well take advantage of our sales tax position but not mention our highest-in-the-nation property taxes.

If this *cost plus 10 percent* concept works in Rochester, it could be copied in every downtown in NH.

43

A SUCCESSFUL *COST PLUS 10 PERCENT* COULD HAVE NATIONWIDE SIGNIFICANCE

Published 3/31/10

This is a follow-up to last week's letter about reviving downtown. While the concept of a fruit and produce or meat retail outlet which could be successful and draw much-needed foot traffic to downtown, the concept of selling 100 percent American made goods at *cost plus 10 percent* could be part of the answer to provide job growth to the American economy through the private sector.

A friend told me what worked 45 years ago could not work today; to which I responded that in professional football, we have hundreds and hundreds of complicated offenses and defenses, but you know what? If a team can't block, their offense wouldn't work, and if they can't tackle, their defense wouldn't work.

I know there are basic fundamentals in business and in sports that have changed in 45 years, but as the French saying goes, "The more things change, the more they remain the same."

In business as well as sports, you must know your competition. Is the competition today more or less than 45 years ago? I think we have more over-saturated markets in America. Money was too easily given to the large corporations to grow their businesses without making profits in many of their new stores. As we all know, growth without profits is false growth.

Many of these retail chains who are in over-saturated marketplaces have diversified their inventories to sell new items while not increasing their overhead.

So yes, retail is more competitive than 45 years ago. That's why foreign countries with slave labor workforces are taking away more American jobs with their $1 or $2 per hour wages. The *cost plus 10 percent* concept will give American made goods more competitive prices in the American marketplace.

Will selling American made goods make our goods cheaper than slave labor countries? No. However, it will level the playing field. Also, female American shoppers will soon realize that a bra made in America retailing at *cost plus 10 percent* for $39 is of better quality and will last twice as long as a foreign made bra that sells for $29. However, if the American made bra sold for $59, the price would win out over the quality.

American made quality is better and will last longer. The *cost plus 10 percent* concept of retailing American manufactured goods will create job growth in America.

To play it safe, I would advise any entrepreneur who would like the challenge of selling American made goods at *cost plus 10 percent* to do an extensive exploratory fact finding inquiry.

First, find the downtown location with the necessary parking. Second, have a low or reasonable rent for one year with the option of five years at a higher rent. The reason for this is if it doesn't create the volume needed to lower costs, they could not renew their lease then sell out their inventory without losing their life savings.

Third would be to get a list from the Rochester Chamber of Commerce of every manufacturer in America who makes 100 percent of the manufactured goods in America. With Chamber cooperation this can be done.

Fourth, select an opening inventory of 500,000 to 1 million good, fast moving items. And then have a grand opening with full page advertisement. With the proper buying and pricing of the goods at *cost plus 10 percent,* little or no further advertising would be necessary.

Of course, this *cost plus 10 percent* concept could be a non-profit organization and have legal fees offered at pro-bono costs.

I truly believe if run properly, this *cost plus 10 percent* ("Buy American; the job you save may be your own") could add job growth and whereas NH doesn't have a sales tax it would exploit our no-sales-tax position.

Another thing we could do is sell large loaves of bread, extra large eggs, gallons of milk only and potatoes by the truckload direct from Maine at *cost plus 10 percent* prices below supermarket everyday prices. Selling those four basic food items 52 weeks a year will bring weekly traffic to the store.

44

MANUFACTURING IS THE KEY TO JOB GROWTH IN AMERICA

Published 4/17/10

When I opened up Signal Street Variety in April of 1985, I had Rochester's largest employer 100 yards from me. Yes, that's the Al-Gore Shoe Company, with their 740 employees that made my grossly undercapitalized retail variety store a success.

It is a proven fact that for any American job in manufacturing, three other jobs are created. We simply can't give our manufacturing jobs away to foreign countries (like China) that employ workers for $1 or $2 per hour.

One way to increase manufacturing jobs in America is to make American-made goods more competitive in price compared to goods sold in America made with a slave labor workforce. Selling American manufactured goods at *cost plus 10 percent* will close the gap in price between American-made goods and foreign-made goods.

With American-made goods being of better quality, American consumers will buy American and gradually revive our manufacturing jobs in America.

If New Balance has shoe factories in America and in China (which they do) and the Chinese made shoes sell for $69 or $79 in America and the New Balance shoes made in America sell for $99 or $109, then many Americans will buy the foreign made shoes. However, if under a *cost plus 10 percent* concept of retailing in America they can sell American-made New Balance shoes for $89 or less, Americans will buy American.

When I think of all the hard workers in the Al-Gore shoe factory losing their jobs because of unfair free world trade, I want to cry. These workers who froze on their jobs in the winter because of inadequate heat and then worked in 100 degree heat in the summer only to be told "You're out of a job because we can't compete in price with shoes made in slave labor countries" is a travesty of justice.

The shoe manufacturing business in America is virtually gone. The furniture manufacturing in America is losing factories every year. When will it end?

In our *cost plus 10 percent* retail store, which sells American-made goods only, we could just show a bedroom set, living room set, recliner, etc., and have a catalog of all the furniture in the American-made factory. A shopper could order anything in the catalog for *cost plus 10 percent* prices.

So in reality, only a sampling of this quality furniture would be on display, but 100 percent of these manufactured goods could be on sale at a *cost plus 10 percent* outlet.

In 1964, I remember going into the post office in Rochester and there was a picture of Lyndon Baines Johnson and under his picture was printed, "You can't have tomorrow's jobs with today's skills. Go to the college of your choice." I mean was this a ridiculous statement or what? It implied that all Americans had to have a college education or there would be no jobs for them in our economy.

This proclamation in 1964 by LBJ was as stupid as Obama telling us that future job growth will come from green jobs. This is also a bunch of bull. Does he mean that China and other slave labor nations participating in the global marketplace are going to give America all those high-paying green jobs?

The first thing America must do to increase job growth is get out of the World Trade Organization (WTO), which is a wealth transfer organization not in the best interests of America, and the only problem with free world trade is that only America practices it.

The second thing America must do is make American-made goods more competitive in price in our own American marketplace by adopting the *cost plus 10 percent* concept of retailing.

With the 50 states in America cutting expenses by cutting jobs, and with the unfair free world trade agreement taking away American jobs, and with the new health care reform, which will be a job killer, America will go into 2011 with a 12 percent unemployment rate and 8 percent not even being counted as they are not included in the unemployment figures.

Why is it that our American government can't work on problems before they become crises? Is it because the large worldwide corporations want to continue making goods worldwide as cheap as possible while selling in America as high as possible and paying as little taxes as possible?

45

THEY HAD GREAT FIRST QUARTER EARNINGS

Published 4/22/10

How come these big ("too big to fail") banks who blackmailed our U.S. Congress for $700 billion (or we would risk a global financial collapse) have great first quarter earnings? These same big banks which made money on risky world investments were privatizing their earnings, with the U.S. taxpayers there to socialize their losses.

Not only did the U.S. taxpayers, with their $700 billion, bail them out of bankruptcy, we stabilized a one percent capital exchange rate so these big banks could have money to lend for investment in America's economy to create job growth.

These big banks took billions of dollars at a one percent rate and bought U.S. treasury notes for three percent. So that gave these big banks money to pay down their $700 billion TARP indebtedness and show a great first quarter profit in January, February and March of this year.

So these big banks paid down their TARP and showed a profit in the first quarter, which gave investors reason to buy their stocks.

By taking this one percent federal money they still couldn't erase the bad debt on their balance sheets, which they will still have to write off.

The "too big to fail" problem is still with us. It is a global problem which can only be solved with a global solution.

If we the American taxpayers are asked in any way, shape or manner to help solve this "too big to fail" problem we must have 100 percent transparency in the assets and liabilities on the balance sheets of these big banks.

The U.S. Congress is now, under the Federal Financial Regulation Reform Act, trying to make new rules and regulations which will not allow another global financial meltdown. This new U.S. financial reform act will not work unless we have global participation.

After the passage of the American Federal Financial Regulation Reform Act and the Volcker Rule legislation we still will have "too big to fail" banks and financial investment firms which will pose systemic risks to our American financial system as well as the world financial system.

46

WE AMERICANS NEED A LOBBYIST

Published 5/2/10

In 1990, our American banking system had successfully weathered the 1988 and 1989 real estate problem before it became a crisis. The FDIC closed many insolvent banks and immediately opened them up under new, solvent banks. Nobody lost any money.

Today, 20 years later, America's 8,200 member banking system is experiencing the same real estate problems. The Federal Deposit Insurance Corporation (FDIC), with their 100 percent transparency of our banks, closed and reopened 140 banks last year and another 50 this year; however, things are still under control.

I hereby want to alert all Americans that our banking system will be inter-related with new world-wide banking regulations coming out of Washington in the next six months.

The big banks have already spent millions on lobbyists to protect their best interests in the Federal Financial Regulation Reform Act (FFRRA) and the Volcker Rule legislation. Goldman Sachs alone spent $290,000 last month.

Along with the banks' lobbyists are the foreign G-20 countries who are watching every aspect of this bill to protect their best interests. The reforms needed could be in a 30-page reform bill; however, when it passes it will be 1,500 or more pages.

Who, pray tell, is looking out for the best interests of America and our domestic banking system?

Being "too big to fail" causes a systemic risk because the whole world-wide financial system is too integrated; that's why we need 100 percent transparency before we let the American taxpayers get sucked in to guaranteeing the debts of any foreign or domestic banks or investment companies.

Do you know who owns Citizens Bank in the U.S.? It's the Royal Bank of Scotland. Do you know who owns 80 percent of the Royal Bank of

Scotland? It's the government of the United Kingdom. Do you know who, in 2008, bought $5 billion worth of shares from Goldman Sachs? A guy named Warren Buffet.

I am just letting my fellow Americans know how integrated all those big banks and investment corporations are.

We, the American people, must, in these new banking regulations, protect our 8,200 member American banking system and let our FDIC take care of our banking systems like we did in 1990.

47

IF I WAS THE CEO OF GOLDMAN SACHS

Published 5/13/10

If I was the CEO of Goldman Sachs, I would never have appeared before the U.S. Congress on national television. These Congressmen, who had no business sense, were only looking to score points with the American people.

The end result of the probing questions asked by these clowns in Washington was political theater at its worst. With e-mails taken out of context, they made Goldman Sachs' CEO defend himself as being guilty of a business transaction that all others in the world-wide banking system are doing.

With only eight percent of U.S. Congressmen being businessmen, they wanted to politically cash in on the public's disdain towards the large banks. Who better than Goldman Sachs?

If these Congressmen's main motive was to cast doubt on Goldman Sachs' operations, they sure did one hell of a job. Goldman Sachs' stock is going down every day, costing many shareholders and pension fund owners great financial losses.

If I was the CEO of Goldman Sachs, I would have declined Congress's invitation to appear before a Congressional hearing. This would be my statement to them:

"I respectfully decline your invitation to appear before Congress. As you know, the Security Exchange Commission (SEC) has, on a vote of 3-2, selected my company, Goldman Sachs, to appear before them to answer our methods of doing business.

"These charges by the SEC are not charges of any illegal transactions and will be explained to the SEC in detail. In America, we all are innocent until proven guilty. After the SEC investigation, I will be more than willing to appear before Congress.

"As you know, Goldman Sachs employs hundreds of thousands of workers world-wide and has billions of investors' dollars that we have to safeguard.

We must show them a reasonable yield on their investment. Goldman Sachs is competing with hundreds of banking and investment institutions for this investment money. We take the obligations very seriously and that is our bottom line.

"Goldman Sachs has done nothing illegal, as the SEC inquiry will prove in the near future. In the meantime, we are, as other big banks and investment corporations are, playing the game as the current laws and regulations are laid out to us. I assure you that when new banking reform comes out of Congress that we, and our competitors, will abide by them. Goldman Sachs is in a rough/tough business, and we didn't get to be number one by worrying if every one of our thousands of daily transactions were ethical or moral. Our job was to make money for our shareholders."

48

WAL-MART IS A MONOPOLY

Published 6/3/10

Having been in the wholesale and retail business for 50 years, I would be the last person to say Wal-Mart doesn't offer us Americans lower prices on just about everything. However, with their thousands of stores in America and in the world, with short-term, cut-throat pricing, they eliminate competition in any given marketing area that they open a new store in.

When they opened their new store in Rochester about 10 years ago, they priced their Marlboros and other name-brand cigarettes at $13.99 a carton. At the time, I had my Marlboros at $14.39 a carton. So on the day they opened, I dropped my price to $13.85 a carton. The next day, they dropped their price to $13.79 a carton. I couldn't believe they were about to get my cigarette business. Knowing that Philip Morris (the manufacturer of Marlboros) was having a $2 a carton promotion coming up, I lowered my Marlboros to my original $14.39 price less $2, making them $12.39.

Guess what? On the same day, Wal-Mart took $2 off their $13.85 price, making theirs $11.85. The next week they were informed of Philip Morris's $2 discount and immediately lowered their Marlboros to $9.89 a carton.

I purchased cigarettes from the Portsmouth Wal-Mart at much higher than they were selling them for in their new Rochester store. I also purchased Marlboros and other name-brand cigarettes at their wholesale Sam's Club in Seabrook. I put the receipts of all my cigarette purchases in the newspaper, showing Rochester Wal-Mart's cut-throat pricing.

I called our cigarette battle a David and Goliath retail fight. However, it was really a Goliath vs. Goliath battle as I was the largest retailer (with my three stores) in New Hampshire.

Anyhow, they finally put their prices up to where mine were, at $14.39 a carton.

When Wal-Mart opens a new store they go after other stores in their marketing area and sell way below cost to run their competitors out of business. More often than not, after Wal-Mart puts their competitors out of business, they put their prices back up to their normal shelf prices.

Wal-Mart has different prices in all their stores, depending on the competition in the area.

Knowing that cut-throat pricing is temporary pricing used to eliminate competition, I proposed a bill to the NH state legislature which would not allow any NH retailers to limit quantities on items that were not in short supply.

My reasoning was cut-throat pricing was short-term pricing used to eliminate long-term competition, which would give Wal-Mart a monopoly with no competition at all.

This well thought-out and well written bill did not even get out of committee. Their reasoning was that the consumers got the benefits of this cut-throat pricing.

One of the reasons Wal-Mart is a monopoly now is that they eliminated competitors with temporary cut-throat pricing when they couldn't do it if they were not allowed to limit quantities.

Today, Wal-Mart is working toward eliminating many of our food retailers. They have thousands of items they can jack up the prices on and then put food prices below costs. Just last week, they put 32 name brand grocery items way below costs in an effort to get the lion's share of the retail food business.

Wal-Mart is a monopoly which will come back to haunt us. They really need a union for they are exploiting their full-time workers with non-union wages and few health benefits.

49

WAL-MART BOSSES URGE THEIR EXECUTIVES TO NOT VOTE FOR DEMOCRATS

Published 8/7/08

It is of their opinion that a Democratic Congress and a Democratic President will be pushing to unionize Wal-Mart. There is no doubt in my mind that having a union in Wal-Mart is long overdue.

Sure, Wal-Mart pays their management above union wages and benefits; they also offer their management incentives to stay and grow with the company. They have to if they want to keep key personnel.

Wal-Mart also hires thousands of senior citizens at $8 or $9 an hour for part-time jobs. Which, by the way, is above minimum wage and is greatly needed and appreciated by an ever-growing number of seniors who have to work part-time to supplement their income (which is not keeping pace with the cost of living).

As the old joke goes, another day another dollar – the only problem today is that it takes a dollar and a quarter to live.

Wal-Mart takes care of their management and their part-time senior citizens, so why do they need a union? Well, I will tell you why.

There are thousands and thousands of Wal-Mart employees who work full-time that do not make union wages or receive full health care benefits, etc., etc. These Wal-Mart workers are in America's lower income bracket. If they were to receive union pay and benefits, they would move up the economic ladder and become middle income workers. They would pay more taxes and purchase more goods and services.

Does Wal-Mart need a union? You bet they do. Is the Democratic Party pro-union? You bet it is.

There are these so-called Conservative Republicans who want to blame the unions for just about everything going wrong in our economy, and to be honest, unions are not without blame. However, unions do more good for the American economy than bad.

Wal-Mart is trying to take over the retail food industry across America. Most all of these established food chains are unionized and have great benefits. If Wal-Mart is not unionized, it will give them a huge advantage over established food chains.

Having been in the wholesale/retail food business, I can tell you first-hand that established national food chains make about one percent net profit after taxes. They cannot afford unfair competition from a *non-union* business like Wal-Mart.

Does Wal-Mart need a union? You bet they do.

50

AMERICA MUST GO ON THE OFFENSE AGAINST TERRORISTS

Published 1/14/10

In a professional football game, there are 60 minutes played. There is a proven oxymoron which states a good offense is a team's best defense. So if a team is playing another team with a great offense, they try to control the ball more than 30 minutes, not allowing their opponent possession of the ball.

Under this scenario, the team who controlled the ball 45 minutes with their offense allows the other team only 15 minutes to allow them to go on their offense. This proves out the theory of a good offense is a team's best defense.

America and all the free world must go on the offense against terrorists and play as little defense against them as possible.

Thank God the near tragedy on Christmas Day was prevented. A plane carrying 282 people nearly exploded, and everyone would have been killed.

If we were on the offense against terrorists the CIA should have, months ago, let the FBI and other law officers get an immediate suspected terrorist subpoena and invaded this supposed terrorist's living quarters with a warrant.

I know in America we are presumed innocent until proven guilty; however, we must consider terrorists guilty until proven innocent.

If I and other Americans have to give up some of our personal freedoms to prevent terrorist acts against innocent men, women and children, then so be it.

Terrorists are not soldiers in a war and do not have any rights to the Geneva Convention or a day in court.

We must reopen the Guantanamo Bay military base in Cuba and let these terrorists rot in hell. Knowing they are not ever getting out of incarceration, they may choose to commit suicide and meet their God early.

I know many Americans and the American Civil Liberties Union (ACLU) will fight this subpoena and warrant demand to go on the offensive against terrorists to stop them before they kill more innocent people.

The Obama Administration, in trying to give terrorists their day in court, is playing defense with terrorists. They deserve no rights, and if I have to give up some of my rights to save innocent people from being killed by cowardly terrorists, that's ok.

We Americans went through World War I, World War II, the Korean War, the Vietnam War, the Iraq War and the Afghanistan War, and with the exception of the World Trade Center bombing on 9/11/01, we have not experienced the ravages of war on our American soil. It's a whole new ballgame now; we must get suspected terrorists off the streets and put them in jail. We need immediate subpoenas and warrants to go on the offense against terrorists.

51

GREECE, SPAIN, PORTUGAL, THE U.S.?

Published 2/18/10

The President released his 2010 budget beginning on Oct. 1st of last year, with total spending of $3.7 trillion and a projected deficit of $1.56 trillion. Because of revenue shortfalls, his 2010 budget will carry a $2 trillion deficit.

Can you imagine a $3.7 trillion budget carrying a $2 trillion deficit? I can't.

Maybe then the Obama administration will realize that the federal government cannot create jobs with astronomical deficit spending.

America is in a rigged poker game called Free World Trade. The chips used in the game are *job chips*. The governments of other countries in this poker game bend and break the rules of the game to win job chips from America. They realize that jobs are the key to a sound economy.

Speaking of jobs, our federal government is reporting weekly unemployment figures which are so complicated that they can be interpreted as positive job growth or negative job growth. I guess they like to fudge up the statistics so the Bulls and Bears can put their own spin on it.

One statistic in the Friday, Feb. 4 job reports was part-time workers who are getting in 34 hours, up from 31.5. Both the Bulls and Bears took this as a positive figure in the job reports. Their wrong assumption was that businesses increase the hours of part-time workers before they hire full-time workers.

The fact of the matter is big and small businesses in America cannot hire full-time workers because of the cost of the health care they will be forced to pay for their full-time employees.

The health care bill in the Senate and the House is an unfunded mandate which will be detrimental to full-time job creation.

52

THE TEA PARTY NEEDS TO OFFER CONSTRUCTIVE CRITICISM

Published 5/27/10

The Tea Party movement in America consists of, for the most part, disgruntled conservative Republicans who feel betrayed by the Bush Administration. They also are very disturbed about the Obama Administration's march toward socialism.

When Aunt Jemima came out with a new syrup, many pancake eaters said, "What took you so long?" I bet you half of those Tea Party members voted for George Bush for a second term. The Tea Party people should have come out four years ago decrying Bush's "deficits don't matter" federal budgets. As Aunt Jemima's fans said, "What took you so long?"

If the Tea Party people want to make a difference in America's upcoming national debt crisis, they must start to offer some constructive criticism to our seemingly unsolvable national debt problems. Unless they can come up with a unified answer to America's upcoming financial crisis, they will be nothing more than political theater for the news media.

Oh yeah, they also need a leader like Mitt Romney or Ron Paul, someone with a business background and name recognition.

Sarah Palin can draw crowds with her anti-Obama rhetoric, but so far I haven't heard her addressing America's great problems.

We don't need a Tea Party platform with no leader to be in denial of world problems and whose only political war cry is "cut spending and cut taxes."

53

THE COFFEE PARTY

Previously Published

I used to be indecisive, but now I'm not quite sure. I know I am still redundant and often repeat myself. I consider myself a leader, but every time I turn around there is nobody behind me.

I have, since 1964, been telling the American people that LBJ's socialistic Great Society programs would lead us to the Welfare Society that we have today.

Several weeks ago I chastised the Tea Party movement as disgruntled Conservative Republicans who were in denial of our grave global problems, and their only political war cry is "cut spending and cut taxes."

I asked why these so-called conservatives voted for Bush a second term. If they were true conservatives they would have formed their Tea Party five years ago, decrying Bush's "deficits don't matter" federal budgets.

Now to change the subject. On Friday, June 4 I read in *Foster's* that on Sunday, June 6 there was a meeting scheduled in Portsmouth of the supposedly new movement in America called the Coffee Party. Their purpose was to have average Americans (like me and you) to talk politics and come up with a consensus of opinions which would offer constructive criticism to our federal government. That is what I have been trying to do for years now.

Well, I am a retired businessman, pushing 80, and suffer from diabetes and depression, so I could not attend this meeting of the NH chapter of the Coffee Party. However, I will send much written information for them to address and take action on.

What I would like to tell the Coffee Party people is that I applaud the goals of their organization. Also, many of America's problems will become crises if action is not started by the end of this year.

The greatest problem is our national debt, which I have written extensively on. So not to be redundant, I am signing off.

Good luck, Coffee Party. You are on the right track.

54

WHAT NEEDS TO BE DONE

Published 1/31/08

First and foremost, we must get out of the WTO (World Trade Organization). It is an organization which is supposed to replace GATT, regulate world trade and lead us to global economic interrogation. It is yet another international bureaucracy whose functionaries will be largely autonomous.

The WTO reports to over 120 nations and therefore, in practice, no nobody. Each nation has one vote out of 120. Thus America will be handing over ultimate control of our economy to an unelected, uncontrolled group of international bureaucrats representing the best interests of large, multinational corporations.

Yes, the WTO is a *wealth* transfer organization, *heavily weighted* against America, and the problem with free world trade is that *only America practices it.*

As it is written, the WTO laws can over-ride our American laws. How our President and Congress can go along with the WTO is beyond me. Could it be that big business money is keeping the U.S. Congress quiet about the WTO, or are they that dumb?

In either case, we must get out of the WTO. It is not good for our economy. It also threatens our national sovereignty and takes away our power to control our own economic destiny.

The second thing America must do to fix our economy is to declare our insolvency. In personal terms, we must declare our insolvency to protect our assets, which mainly is our $14 trillion economy.

America owes over $6 trillion, mostly to foreign countries, and about $3 trillion to our Social Security surplus. America paid $327 billion in interest on our debt as of Sept. 30th in fiscal year 2005, $406 billion in interest on our debt in the 2006 fiscal year, and nearly $500 billion on our debt in interest in the fiscal year 2007.

President Bush's deficits don't matter; economic policies since he was elected in 2000 have literally bankrupted the U.S. If deficits didn't matter, how come the interest on our debt went up from $327 billion to $406 billion, to $500 billion?

What America must do is freeze our U.S. treasury bonds and only allow 10 percent to be withdrawn per year. Naturally, U.S. bond holders will get interest on the frozen bonds they own.

Japan, China, South Korea, some oil rich mid-east countries, etc., etc., have U.S. Treasury notes payable on demand. So, in essence, the foreign countries who hold U.S. Treasury notes can push the U.S. into bankruptcy. Of course, they don't want to do this because they will be killing the U.S. economy, which they so much depend upon.

Foreign countries have a minimum of $5 trillion which they can invest in America. We must make sure these investments do not threaten our national security or monopolize our economy.

The U.S. dollars that foreign countries have to invest in America are not the immediate problem facing America. The immediate problem is that America cannot provide the liquidity needed to China or any other country who wants to cash in their U.S. Treasury notes.

China has devalued their currency by about 40 percent, which allows them to drain billions of dollars from America with their trade imbalance with the U.S., plus the interest we pay them on our national debt. China has about a trillion in cash to invest in America or world-wide. However, it is the $450 billion U.S. Treasury notes which they hold over our head when we try to bargain for fair trade with them.

In order to get *fair world trade,* which will provide the good jobs we need in our American economy, we must freeze our treasury notes and balance the American budget while paying down on our national debt.

China and every other foreign country still needs America's $14 trillion economy as much as we need them. We must put a 40 percent tariff on all Chinese imports until they stop devaluing their currency by 40 percent.

There are a lot of other things America must do to receive fair trade in the world-wide marketplace; however, freezing our treasury notes is the first big step.

The first argument the millions of intellectuals we have in America will say is the 40 percent tariff on Chinese imports will be highly inflationary.

If I am one of the millions of Americans who can't afford to put food on the table, put gas in the car, or heat their home in the winter and pay their taxes, I don't care if Chinese imports go up.

It is my opinion that when we put this 40 percent tariff on Chinese imports they will stop devaluing their currency by 40 percent. We have got to start playing hardball with China if we are going to break the stranglehold they have on our economy.

55

W.O.P. MEANS WITHOUT PAPERS

Published 4/23/08

My father and mother immigrated to America from the northern part of Italy as children. They went through Ellis Island and were stamped W.O.P., which meant *without papers.* So I guess technically they were illegal. At least they didn't change my father's first name to *Tony* and ship him to New York.

Seriously, we all know the part immigrants played in building the great United States of America. The problem we have in America today is not with immigration but with illegal immigration. We must secure our own borders with Mexico and Canada, then set up an Ellis Island Building to process illegal immigrants as soon as possible into American citizens who pay all taxes, their own educational costs, and their own health care costs.

Once we secure our borders and start processing new American citizens, we must deal with the 16 to 20 million illegals we have living in America today.

One must remember the majority of hard working, law abiding illegals are assets to the American economy if they become citizens.

I say if they have a steady job for one year they can become naturalized citizens within six months. This way U.S. law enforcement can sort out the newly made U.S. citizens from the illegal criminals.

Of course we will have to raise the minimum wage about $2 per hour and of course the newly made citizens would probably have to work two or three jobs (like the rest of our lower income and middle income Americans).

We must not continue to let big business (National Chamber of Commerce), etc., etc., bring in illegal workers and not pay them a living wage.

Other American citizens are being taxed to subsidize their education, health care, and costs of increased law enforcement.

It's time we American citizens realize being an American citizen isn't the big deal it used to be. Most Americans are poor, lower income, and middle income, are in debt or living from paycheck to paycheck.

America needs hard working, law abiding citizens who want to live the American Dream even if it takes the whole family to do it.

Will my solution to illegal immigration be fair to all? Hell no, but who said life was fair?

Also, if we don't enforce the borders, terrorists can walk right into the United States of America.

www.ingramcontent.com/pod-product-compliance
Lightning Source LLC
Chambersburg PA
CBHW051431280526
45785CB00003B/1247